Improving Teacher Quality
A Guide for Education Leaders

Sabrina Laine with Ellen Behrstock-Sherratt and Molly Lasagna

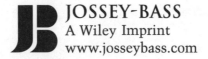

JOSSEY-BASS
A Wiley Imprint
www.josseybass.com

Published by Jossey-Bass
A Wiley Imprint
989 Market Street, San Francisco, CA 94103-1741—www.josseybass.com

Jossey-Bass books and products are available through most bookstores. To contact Jossey-Bass directly call our Customer Care Department within the U.S. at 800-956-7739, outside the U.S. at 317-572-3986, or fax 317-572-4002.

Jossey-Bass also publishes its books in a variety of electronic formats. Some content that appears in print may not be available in electronic books.

Library of Congress Cataloging-in-Publication Data

Laine, Sabrina W. M.
    Improving teacher quality: a guide for education leaders / Sabrina Laine with Ellen Behrstock-Sherratt and Molly Lasagna.
        p. cm.
    Includes bibliographical references and index.
    ISBN 978-0-470-58590-0 (pbk.)
            9780470933732   ePDF
            9780470933749   eMobi
            9780470933756   ePub
    1. Teacher effectiveness.   2. Teachers–Rating of.   3. Performance standards.   I. Behrstock-Sherratt, Ellen.   II. Lasagna, Molly.   III. Title.
    LB1025.3.L35 2011
    371.2'03–dc22

                                                                2010040025

Printed in the United States of America
FIRST EDITION

PB Printing   10 9 8 7 6 5 4 3 2 1

Contents

Figures and Rubrics

The Authors

Sabrina W. M. Laine, PhD, is chief program officer for educator quality at Learning Point Associates. She manages the National Comprehensive Center for Teacher Quality funded by the U.S. Department of Education and is a principal investigator for the Center for Educator Compensation Reform. Laine has a diverse background in educational policy research and has spearheaded efforts to contribute to policy research and resource development related to every aspect of managing and supporting educator talent, including recruitment, compensation, evaluation, distribution, and professional development. She leads a team of more than fifteen researchers and policy analysts who are focused on the challenges faced by educators in urban, rural, and low-performing schools. She has worked for the last several years to ensure that policies and programs are in place that enable all children to gain access to highly qualified teachers and leaders. Laine earned her doctorate in educational leadership and policy studies from Indiana University.

Ellen J. Behrstock-Sherratt, PhD, is a policy associate at Learning Point Associates. Her area of focus is teacher quality and school leadership. Behrstock led the development of the Managing Educator Talent (METworks^{SM}) Framework, allowing districts and states to identify gaps between their current practices for managing educator talent and the elements of effective practice identified in the research. She has authored or coauthored articles and briefs on topics such as strategies for supporting Generation Y teachers, teachers' use of educational research, innovations in state-level teacher quality policies, teacher compensation, and teacher and administrator induction. Behrstock-Sherratt also presented and facilitated discussions at National Comprehensive Center for Teacher Quality conferences and issue forums and has provided technical assistance to a collaborative of New England states relating to defining and measuring educator effectiveness. Behrstock-Sherratt earned her doctoral degree in education from the University of Oxford.

Molly S. Lasagna is a policy associate at Learning Point Associates. Her work in educator quality focuses on conducting high-quality research and evaluations and disseminating the results through multiple media to diverse audiences in the public education sector. She contributes to initiatives of the Center for Educator Compensation Reform and the National Comprehensive Center for Teacher Quality. Previously, Lasagna worked at the Nellie Mae Education Foundation, where she was a program associate for Pathways to Higher Learning. She also taught middle school language arts in Richmond, Virginia, for three years. Lasagna earned a master's degree in secondary English education from the University of Virginia and a master's degree in urban education policy from Brown University.

Improving Teacher Quality

Introduction

It's the first day of school, but amidst the excitement is the uncomfortable knowledge that, yet again, some students will be deprived of excellent teachers this year. You feel you did everything within your power to deliver the teaching talent students need. Nevertheless, despite your efforts to convince them otherwise, several of the best teachers are leaving while the handful of teachers who seem consistently unable to get through to their students have no plans to improve their practice or move on. Meanwhile, well-intentioned parents are pulling you in one direction, legal and district requirements in another, and your conscience is telling you that the one solution that will let you sleep at night is to recruit, retain, and develop enough highly effective teachers for each and every student. But how do you do it?

Some things never change. A sixteenth-century English knight by the name of Sir Thomas Elyot wrote: "The chief cause, why in our time noble men be not as excellent in learning, as they were in old time among the Romans and Greeks [is]... *the lack or fewness of sufficient masters or teachers*" (Elyot, 1557, p. 36).

Twenty-first-century education in the United States has advanced considerably since medieval times, but the concern about the number and quality of teachers persists. Although some researchers and education leaders argue that these worries are the mere grumblings of alarmists and that in fact there are more teachers seeking jobs than classrooms needing teachers, other stakeholders remain convinced that shortfalls of sufficiently high-quality teachers are leading to inequities and poor outcomes in the education and life opportunities of many children (Akiba, LeTendre, & Scribner, 2007; Antonucci, 2009; Darling-Hammond, 2006).

There is consensus among researchers and education leaders at every level of the education system that teachers are the most important school-level factor affecting student achievement. In addition to the obvious role of teachers in improving children's academic growth, other societal concerns— from crime to health to economic competitiveness to democracy itself—are affected by the formal and informal learning that takes place in schools.

For this reason, concerned individuals and organizations across many stakeholder groups have felt compelled to take action to attract and retain teachers who are highly competent, caring, and committed to student success. Unfortunately, such teachers still are not available for all students or for all subjects. Poor and minority children, in particular, are systematically taught by teachers with less experience and fewer credentials (Imazeki & Goe, 2009).

This book discusses research and concrete practices that education leaders can use to improve teacher quality by focusing on teacher recruitment and retention. As the role of school principal has evolved from one of manager to instructional leader, the importance of teacher recruitment, retention, and development has become a more central priority among the many responsibilities of principals. What the principal does or does not do has become a key influence on teachers' levels of satisfaction with their choice of profession or school and their effectiveness in promoting student learning. At the same time, though, the principal cannot be solely responsible for creating the types of practices and conditions that teachers need. The support of school districts, unions, institutions of higher education, state departments of education and state policymakers is equally important.

In this book, we present strategies and promising practices spanning various policy areas that influence the overall quality of teachers and each of the key groups with a stake in education reform. Whereas most other books on this topic focus on one educator policy area (for example, preparation or professional development) and address a more limited audience, this book places the principal at the heart of teacher recruitment and retention, yet aims to be relevant to all concerned parties. So whether you are from a state education agency, a school district office, a university, a union or advocacy group, or any number of other groups concerned with teacher quality, you will gain insights on how to shape policies that will secure the teaching talent that principals need to deliver a high-quality education for all students. If you are a school principal, this book will shed light both on what you can do in your school to improve teacher quality *and* on how you can work with the wider educational community to facilitate the types of reforms and supports that are needed to ensure that all of your students are taught by effective teachers.

This approach is adopted because no one stakeholder group can realize lasting change on its own. Likewise, reform initiatives focusing on just one type of strategy cannot create the workplace conditions needed to truly build capacity within the education profession. Rather, collaboration and common understanding and purpose are needed among all stakeholders, and their priorities must include progress along a number of critical avenues that may crucially affect children's access to high-quality teachers.

A SYSTEMIC APPROACH TO HUMAN CAPITAL MANAGEMENT

A systemic approach to human capital management—or *educator talent-management,* as we refer to it in this book—addresses the entire continuum of teacher policies and practices, as well as the relevant stakeholder groups with a stake in ensuring a highly effective teaching faculty. A systemic approach ensures that all of the pieces and all of the players are strategically aligned and not working at cross-purposes. In looking at the "system" for attracting and retaining teachers, our intention is to offer greater perspective, greater ownership of change, and greater access to innovative ideas and best practice to individuals whose jobs typically allow them to see only certain aspects of teacher quality reforms. The "systemic" approach is meant to better equip education leaders to influence the broader realm of teacher quality reforms.

Current practice in education often treats the securing of "human capital" talent in a passive manner (Maxwell, 2008). In *The State of Education Policy Research*, Odden, Milanowski, and Heneman (2007) note that "although strategic human resource management has been emphasized in other sectors, in the field of education its potential to improve teacher quality has received little attention" (p. 340). Lynn Olson (2008), then executive editor of *Education Week,* stated that in practice in education there is "no system for attracting, training, and supporting the best people for the job."

Compared to other sectors, education lags behind. Where other industries refer to a "war for talent" (MacMillan, 2008), the education field is far more subdued in its campaign for more high-quality teachers and its actions to meet this goal. A joint study by IBM Corporation and the Human Capital Institute found that although attention to human capital practices varied substantially across industries, *the education field was found to be the least likely to engage in "enlightened talent management practices"* (Ringo, Schweyer, DeMarco, Jones, & Lesser, 2008, p. 9).

Education and government lag behind all these industries: banking, retail, financial markets, health care, telecommunications, professional services, industrial products, electronics or technology, and consumer products. It is interesting to note that the industries that engage in the most human capital activities (for example, electronics or technology and professional services) are referred to as the "knowledge-intensive industries," while education is not (Ringo et al., 2008, p. 4).

Teacher recruitment and retention have been policy concerns for many years. The comprehensive and strategic approach to educator talent management initiatives has only recently begun to gain momentum. Recent changes and initiatives within education are currently underway to improve the management of educator talent. For example, the creation of human capital or talent management directorship positions and initiatives in many of the United States' largest school districts reflects recognition of the need for more oversight of the relevant policies and practices for securing a sufficient number of high-quality teachers. These individuals are charged with securing the highest quality teaching force possible by working full-time to oversee the various policies that aim to attract top talent to the district. They break down silos within the district and help stakeholders take a "bird's-eye" view of reform efforts underway, rather than getting stuck in the "worm's-eye" perspective of daily crises. Smaller districts also are concerned with creating the appropriate mix of incentives to maintain a strong teaching force for their students.

In addition, the Strategic Management of Human Capital (SMHC) initiative at the Consortium for Policy Research in Education embarked on an effort to dramatically improve student achievement by strategically improving teacher and administrator recruitment, retention, and development. The initiative focused on the one hundred largest urban districts in the United States and resulted in a series of case studies and a national reform network (Center for Policy Research in Education, n.d.). Learning Point Associates, a nonprofit education consulting organization with a longstanding focus on educator quality, is another national educational organization that systematically has summarized the findings of the large body of literature on teacher and school leader policies in its Managing Educator Talent (METworks[SM]) Framework (Behrstock, Meyer, Wraight, & Bhatt, 2009). The organization has developed a variety of tools, including a state policy inventory and district assessment, to assist education leaders in taking a more comprehensive and deliberate approach to securing enough teachers and school leaders.

This systemic approach to improving teacher quality is in contrast to the more piecemeal, silver-bullet approach that often is seen in education. Some education leaders are convinced that higher pay is the key to a stronger profession; others maintain that stronger preparation programs, alternative routes, high-quality induction, or ongoing professional development represent the missing bridge between where the profession is and where it needs to be. Because teachers affect what is most important to a large majority of members of society—their children—opinions on the appropriate means of improving teaching are both strong and widespread across society.

It appears, then, that teacher quality may remain at the forefront of ongoing national policy conversations not because education leaders have been unable to pinpoint a solution, but because they have identified *too many* uncoordinated solutions, each with the most passionate of advocates backing it as the most important solution. The result is a confused and incoherent policy agenda, along with conflict at the expense of collaboration in moving teacher quality policies; hence the quality of education that children receive suffers. In this book we aim to represent in a comprehensive yet digestible fashion the crucial policy levers that should be tapped in order to better recruit and retain high-quality teachers for all students and the roles of different groups in promoting change.

ABOUT THE METworks^{SM} FRAMEWORK

The components of educator quality policy addressed here are based on the Managing Educator Talent (METworks^{SM}) Framework developed by Learning Point Associates. They include the following eight components, which span the teacher career continuum (these same components apply to principals and other school leaders, but this book primarily focuses on the management of *teacher* talent):

- **Preparation.** Institutions of higher education (IHEs) must be encouraged to ensure that their teacher preparation programs be *selective* in their admissions process and *responsive* to local needs for teachers in certain subjects. IHEs should use a wide variety of pedagogical approaches to develop skills and knowledge applicable to a diverse range of schools and classes and collect data on the effectiveness of their approaches.

- **Recruitment.** District and state officials must actively *determine* and then *market* the positive characteristics of the profession and of teaching in districts where highly effective teachers are in shortest supply. Districts should maintain *high standards* for recruitment while reaching out to diverse potential pools of new teachers.

- **Hiring.** Streamlined hiring processes that operate on an *early hiring timeline* should be in place. Districts and school leaders involved in the hiring process should facilitate a process of *rich information sharing* between districts and applicants to find the best match between applicants and positions.

- **Induction.** A *high-quality induction* and mentoring program that begins before the start of the school year and involves the training of mentors should be available to all new teachers. Districts and school leaders also should ensure *appropriate and manageable* teaching assignments that recognize the novice status of new teachers.

- **Professional development.** *Ongoing job-embedded and differentiated* professional development should be available for all teachers. A range of relevant topics should be offered (for example, classroom management and subject-specific pedagogy), and the type of professional development that individual teachers receive should be based in part on the results of their evaluations.

- **Compensation and incentives.** Teachers should be rewarded *generously,* with salaries that are *market sensitive, competitive, and performance based.* Districts should work closely with all stakeholder groups to develop salary policies that are attractive to their most effective teachers.

- **Working conditions.** Teachers' professional workplace should include *positive, collaborative, and team-oriented* school cultures. School leaders should work to ensure that discipline and classroom management problems are limited, facilities are *safe, clean, and appropriately equipped*, and workloads for teachers are *reasonable.*

- **Performance management.** Teachers' evaluations should be *differentiated* and provide *clear and timely* feedback. School and district leaders should systematically *link* evaluations to teachers' goals, to their professional development, and to incentives.

These components are illustrated in Figure I.1.

Each of these components is necessary, though insufficient on its own, for authentic improvements to teacher recruitment and retention. Each component also must be understood in relation to the others. For example, preparation should transition seamlessly to a comprehensive induction program, which should be aligned with ongoing professional development throughout an educator's career. Professional development must be directly responsive to the performance management system, such that educators' evaluations lead to genuine growth and improvements in effectiveness when it comes to enhancing student learning. At the same time, compensation and other incentives should be linked in some manner to a teacher's development as a professional. These interconnections are shown in Figure I.2.

Figure I.1. Educator Talent Management Components

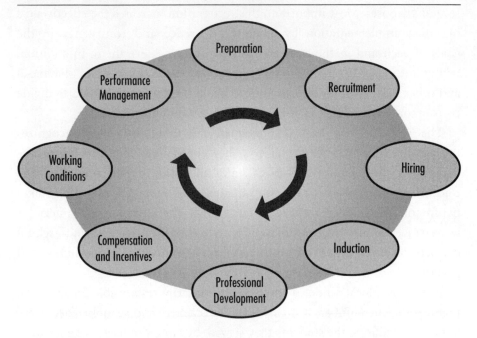

Figure I.2. Educator Talent Management Intercomponent Connections

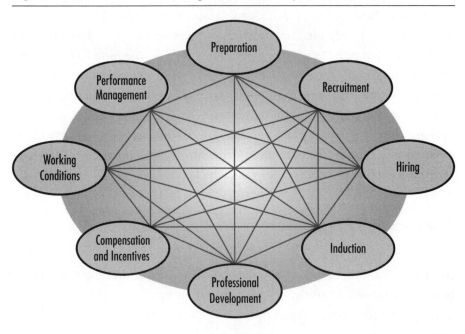

Recognizing the connections between the eight key components serves several purposes. Most important, this recognition increases the effectiveness of policy implementation by creating coherence and consistency in the goals of each and in the strategies developed to achieve them. In addition, taking into account these interconnections creates efficiencies. Financial and other resources can be leveraged to avoid overlap in effort and to divide costs among resources set aside to achieve common purposes.

The systemic approach described in this book not only recognizes the various relevant teacher-quality policy components but also accommodates the critical responsibilities of states and other organizations in what traditionally has been a locally controlled issue. The increasingly high-stakes nature of education reform combined with the complex machinery of governance requires the coordination of state education agencies, local school districts, teachers' unions, institutions of higher education, legislatures, and governors.

In the past, local school districts were primarily responsible for ensuring that a sufficient number of highly effective teachers and school leaders were available to educate the students they served. But in more recent years, and in particular with the 2001 No Child Left Behind Act, the roles and responsibilities of states have increased. For example, states are required to monitor the distribution of highly qualified teachers in their states and, where problems exist, to develop plans to address them. More recently, the American Recovery and Reinvestment Act of 2009, with its $100 billion dedicated to education, encourages states to work innovatively to improve teacher effectiveness. In many ways, the decisions made at the state level either constrain or enable options for school districts. In particular, low-income school districts working to improve educator recruitment and retention are influenced by resource allocation decisions made by state policy makers.

ABOUT THIS BOOK

Incorporating into one resource the multiple critical teacher-quality policy components and the range of key stakeholder groups addressing them serves multiple purposes. Namely, it aids understanding, collaboration, and the development of a shared vision in meeting the highly important educational goal of securing effective teachers for all students. We aim to equip readers with forward-thinking, innovative strategies that are based on research and emerging best practice, thereby motivating readers to take proactive, strategic, and coordinated action.

Securing sufficient quantities of high-quality teachers for all students requires the purposeful collaboration of many participants within the education field, including school leaders, district administrators, institutions of higher education, state education agencies, and unions. This book is structured to highlight strategies and promising practices across the teacher career continuum, from the perspectives of the various parties concerned. Throughout the book you will see vignettes that present real-life examples of how these various players have moved teacher quality policy and practice forward in a meaningful way. Chapter One explores the management of educator talent within schools. The chapter focuses on teachers' working conditions, arguably the most important issue in terms of its influence on teacher attrition. Chapter Two examines the critical role of school districts, which both historically and to this day exert the greatest influence on teacher recruitment and retention. School districts' role in managing all aspects of teacher-talent acquisition and development is addressed, with an emphasis on the recruitment and hiring decisions that do—or, in some cases, do not—ensure that schools "get the right people on the bus."

Chapter Three highlights the role of teachers' unions, including examples of bold new initiatives developed in partnership with districts with the intent of advancing the teaching profession. Traditionally, a key concern of teachers' unions has been the professional pay of teachers. This important, but often controversial, policy component is addressed along with discussion of approaches for effectively evaluating teachers. Chapter Four turns to the role of state and federal government in building capacity within the profession. Chapter Five visits institutions of higher education and their role in equipping new teachers with the skills and knowledge they will need to be effective. Finally, the book concludes with a review of the many strategies introduced in this text as well as the interconnections between and among them so that the relevant stakeholder groups can come together to advance teacher-quality policies that meet and exceed the world-class, twenty-first-century education system that all children need and deserve.

After reading this book you will emerge with a greater understanding of the range of teacher quality policies and the many stakeholder groups that contribute to the policy process. You will be better equipped to lead collaborative work that results in a more effective teaching force and more successful learners. In addition, you will gain a more systemic, big-picture perspective of the existing work taking place across the country to improve teacher quality and improve tangible learning outcomes for all students.

REFERENCES

Akiba, M., LeTendre, G., & Scribner, J. (2007). Teacher quality, opportunity gap, and national achievement in 46 countries. *Educational Researcher 36*(7), 369–387.

Antonucci, M. (2009, December 18). The Yogi Berra logic of California's "teacher shortage." *Educationnews.org*. Retrieved January 22, 2010, from http://www .educationnews.org/blogs/10999.html.

Behrstock, E., Meyer, C., Wraight, S., & Bhatt, M. (2009). *Managing educator talent: A research-based framework for district and state policymakers* (Version 2.1). Naperville, IL: Learning Point Associates.

Center for Policy Research in Education (n.d.). *Strategic Management of Human Capital*. Retrieved March 9, 2009, from http://www.smhc-cpre.org.

Darling-Hammond, L. (2006). Securing the right to learn: Policy and practice for powerful teaching and learning. *Educational Researcher 35*(7), 13–24.

Elyot, T. (1557). *The boke named the governour*. London: Octavius Graham Gilchrist.

Imazeki, J., & Goe, L. (2009). *The distribution of highly qualified, experienced teachers: Challenges and opportunities*. Washington, DC: National Comprehensive Center for Teacher Quality. Retrieved December 1, 2009, from http://www.tqsource.org/ publications/August2009Brief.pdf.

MacMillan, D. (2008, August 13). Talent management: How to invest in your workforce. *BusinessWeek*. Retrieved February 5, 2009, from http://www .businessweek.com/managing/content/aug2008/ca20080813_954038.htm.

Maxwell, L. A. (2008, December 1). Human capital key worry for reformers. *Education Week*, *28*(14), 1, 13. Retrieved February 6, 2009, from http://www.edweek.org/ew/ articles/2008/12/03/14human_ep.h28.html?tmp=1540450504.

Odden, A. R., Milanowski, A., & Heneman, H. G. (2007). Policy and professionals: Commentary. In S. H. Fuhrman, D. K. Cohen, & F. Mosher (Eds.), *The State of Education Policy Research* (pp. 337–348). New York: Routledge.

Olson, L. (2008). Human resources a weak spot. *Education Week*. January 10, 2008. Retrieved November 4, 2008, from http://www.edweek.org/ew/articles/2008/ 01/10/18overview.h27.html?print=1.

Ringo, T., Schweyer, A., DeMarco, M., Jones, R., & Lesser, E. (2008). *Integrated talent management. Part 3—Turning talent management into a competitive advantage: An industry view*. Somers, NY: IBM Corporation. Retrieved February 6, 2009, from http://www.humancapitalinstitute.org/hci/IBM_2008_Part3.dbprop.

CHAPTER ONE

Teachers and Leaders in Schools

The Conditions That Support Effective Teachers and Leaders

Generally, your teachers are satisfied. Their attendance rate is solid, their participation in meetings is active, and overall the students are faring well on the state assessments. Still, you get the sense that things could be better. Is there some reform, some promising practice or innovative idea out there that could transform your faculty from a content one to an enthusiastic one? What improved working conditions do you need to have in place to turn your school into a mission-driven, highly successful exemplar in the district?

OVERVIEW

Prior to strategizing about teacher staffing, evaluation, compensation, or retention, school leaders must first consider *working conditions,* defined as the conditions pertaining to one's place of employment. Promoting high-quality working conditions within a school is like setting the stage for a successful performance. Working conditions encompass many workplace attributes, but one thing is certain: without a principal's thoughtful approach to ensuring strong and positive working conditions, even the brightest and most effective teacher will falter. Susan Moore Johnson (2006), director of the Project on the Next Generation of Teachers, cites poor working conditions as the top reason teachers report leaving a particular school or even the profession altogether. Similar to professionals in other sectors, teachers are far more likely to stay in education if they believe they are being effective in their jobs. Ensuring safe and pleasant working conditions is an important way of enabling practitioners to do their jobs well and to remain committed to teaching.

Through the years, teachers have been very articulate about the workplace attributes that they believe to be essential to their success and professional well-being. In a 2008 survey of all secondary teachers in North Carolina, the following were ranked as the top variables that are critical to increased teacher retention:

- Overall perception of the school being a good place to work and learn
- The effectiveness of the School Improvement Team
- The presence of an atmosphere of trust and mutual respect
- The ability of leaders to shield teachers from disruptions (North Carolina's Teacher Working Conditions Initiative, 2008)

The North Carolina findings are corroborated by a large body of literature on working conditions, which consistently identifies a positive school culture, leadership, access to ongoing professional support, assistance with student discipline, reduced workload for new teachers, and a safe and clean school building as key aspects of a high-functioning workplace. Although some of these conditions are purely a matter of creating an open and trusting atmosphere, others—such as facility upgrades and reduced class sizes—require substantial resources.

In many ways, working conditions relate to nearly every other component along the educator's career continuum. Preparation programs can improve an educator's working conditions by teaching skills to cope with student behavioral problems. Induction programs can ease a new educator's transition into a school and community culture (American Federation of Teachers, 2000). Performance management can build trust among educators and create a working environment in which teachers are constantly growing professionally (Gimbel, 2003). If school leaders can think systemically about improving working conditions for their staff, they are on the road to an effective and efficient structure for successfully managing their teaching talent.

A systemic approach to improving teacher quality considers all of the components along the career continuum, and there are many factors to consider. Some of these are not generated within the school building itself. To begin, consider the following strategies for school- and district-level leaders to create a positive school climate:

- Create a positive, collaborative, and team-oriented school culture that facilitates effective teaching.
- Engage families and the community in a meaningful and genuine way.
- Ensure that teachers' workloads are reasonable.
- Ensure that schools are safe, clean, and appropriately equipped for effective teaching.

This list is by no means exhaustive, but it provides some initial guidance to principals and other school leaders as they seek ways to create positive working conditions for their teachers.

CREATE A POSITIVE, COLLABORATIVE, AND TEAM-ORIENTED SCHOOL CULTURE THAT FACILITATES EFFECTIVE TEACHING

Everyone likes to feel good about going to work. A young professional wants to get up every morning filled with a sense of pride in her workplace. She desires to feel fulfilled with her choice of career and to feel that she is making a difference. For a teacher like Sarah Fine, the postcollege decision to pursue teaching is an easy one. In her article "Why I Left Teaching Behind," Fine (2009) explained:

> When I was a first-year teacher fresh out of college, I got a lot of questions about my chosen profession. I usually said that I was inspired by my grandmother, who taught in the Boston public schools for 35 years. The real truth was that, like many of my peers, I had fallen in love with the idea of the job. Urban classrooms struck me as seductively gritty, and it only seemed right that I "give back" after spending 22 years in a suburban, Ivy League bubble. I rarely voiced this sentiment because I was afraid of sounding cavalier [p. 1].

For a while, teachers can subsist on their passion for teaching alone, or a love of children, or the satisfaction derived from knowing that their students are learning.

In reality, though, the profession of teaching is far too stressful and complex for people to stay on board based on this idealized view of the intrinsic rewards. When students are not listening, parents are not returning phone calls, and administrators are not providing adequate guidance and support, many teachers will reconsider their options. Further on in her article, Fine attempts to explain just what it was about the poor working conditions at Cesar Chavez Elementary School that finally did her in: "More and more major decisions were made behind closed doors, and more and more teachers felt micromanaged rather than supported. One afternoon this spring, when my often apathetic 10th-graders were walking eagerly around the room as part of a writing assignment, an administrator came in and ordered me to get the class 'seated and silent.' It took everything I had to hold back my tears of frustration" (p. 1).

Her experience supports that of many teachers who have left the profession, citing feelings of isolation and underappreciation (Fine, 2009). In addition, although teachers do not view higher compensation as a reason *not* to become a teacher, the lack of opportunity for career advancement combined with a low salary for beginning teachers does influence their decisions to leave the profession—especially when the working conditions in a school or district also are not ideal.

The good news, though, is that school culture can change. Principals and other school leaders can work together to envision a learning environment for both students and teachers that is positive and responsive. When teachers feel supported by their administrators, they are much more likely to persevere through the tough times (Coggshall, Ott, Behrstock, & Lasagna, 2009). A culture of collaboration, caring, and teamwork within a school can mitigate those feelings of isolation that teachers often express and can help teachers to feel that their hard work is appreciated, which ultimately can lead to increased retention among a faculty. Much as Principal Cathy Tomon did in Newport, North Carolina, whose story is shared in the next vignette, it is possible to transform your school into a collaborative, inspired working environment that ultimately results in more effective teaching and learning.

Thinking Outside the Bowl

Effects of the North Carolina Working Conditions Survey

When Cathy Tomon became the principal of Broad Creek Middle School in Newport, North Carolina, she knew that she wanted to bring a fresh, innovative approach to improving working conditions for her faculty and staff. As she began to strategize, she drew from two sources of inspiration: the North Carolina Working Conditions Survey and a fish market. The Working Conditions Survey, which Cathy and her team use to develop their School Improvement Plan each year, is broken into five domains, each of which includes teacher-identified areas in need of improvement. Using this same model, Cathy solicits advice and insight from her teachers regarding the structures and supports they would like to see in place in their work environment. Reaching out to the teachers in this way has had several beneficial outcomes.

To begin, the Broad Creek faculty members requested to be treated more like professionals, a desire often communicated within the teaching world. To this end, Cathy and her fellow administrators made major real-locations of time and resources to better meet the needs of the teachers and, in the end, positively affect student engagement and achievement. "It's funny," she said, "we talk about all the Fs in middle school. For us, we say *family first*, because if you can't take care of your family, how are you expected to take care of these children who don't have a support system at home? We say you have to have *fun*, you have to be *fair*, and you have to be *flexible*. We have to look at grants to get teachers *free* materials." Promising to stay true to the "family first" mantra, Cathy holds no faculty meetings after the last bell of the day. When asked if the teachers were willing to sacrifice some of their planning time to attend these meetings, she answered, "Absolutely." Cathy also implemented a system of peer observation and learning at Broad Creek, which helped to increase trust among the faculty and elevate the school to a National Schools to Watch school, a learning lab for other middle school faculties to visit and learn from. Teachers on Cathy's staff have come to trust and believe in each other so much that now many of the students' projects are created, implemented, and evaluated cross-content. If a student has a project for science class on a famous scientist, for example, that student's language arts teacher will grade the writing, the social studies teacher will grade the quality of the research, and the science teacher will grade the reliability of the science vocabulary.

As far as fiscal resources go, Principal Tomon bucked tradition and embraced the future, transferring $40,000 from her textbook budget to purchase SmartBoards, ELMO projectors, GPS systems, and other pieces of cutting-edge education technology. She goes out of her way to make sure that *all* of her teachers understand and use this technology to its maximum effectiveness. Once a month, Cathy runs a teacher-enrichment program called Tech in 20. "It's once a month, and it's after school, and all you have to give us is twenty minutes of your time. In that twenty minutes, we're going to teach you *something* new using technology. And the teachers are open to it. They know that if they want to continue teaching here, they have to be willing to evolve." She finds that asking the teachers to make this manageable commitment to their own professional development has resulted in gains for both the students and the teachers. When asked about visible results from initiatives such as this, Cathy related the story of a teacher who had traveled to Washington, D.C., recently and wanted his students to be able to share his experience. "One of our teachers was asked by CNN Student News to present at a conference in Washington, D.C., this past year, and while he was there we were able to bring the kids together with him in our telecommunications room. They saw him and what he was doing, and he was able to engage with them. So now, with the cost of field trips being so high, our kids can take virtual field trips where *everybody* can go, not just the kids who can normally afford it. Everybody can get involved."

And then there is the fish market. At the beginning of Cathy's tenure as principal, she wanted to be able to see her teachers having fun at work, believing that the students would enjoy themselves only if the teachers did. After reading the book *Fish! A Remarkable Way to Boost Morale and Improve Results*, Cathy took such strong lessons from the employees of Pike Place Fish Market in Seattle that she journeyed west and spent a week with them, beginning to understand the working conditions that are necessary to make even fishmongers love their jobs day in and day out. "If these guys can love selling fish, my teachers can love to teach," she thought to herself. That year, she decided to make "Think Outside the Bowl" the school motto. In subsequent years, the Broad Creek team has stayed with the aquatic theme, exemplifying the following elements:

- Swimming upstream
- Swimming into open waters
- Not letting the waves hold you back

Just as these sayings are representative of perseverance and determination, the teachers of Broad Creek Middle School are the embodiment of such vibrancy and tenacity. They work to engage parents and guardians before the school year even starts; every parent is asked to write a letter telling about his or her child, and every teacher makes ten phone calls to parents before the second week of school, celebrating students' behaviors or academic achievements. Every teacher has an open-door policy with students, working to get to know them beyond the level of just an academic profile. Each teacher at Broad Creek adopts one at-risk student per year, becoming a hybrid mentor and facilitator of services for that child. The teacher will e-mail to check in, Cathy explained, and also have lunch with his or her mentee and work to engage the necessary support services, such as high-quality school supplies or apparel for gym class. The attitude of reaching out is so prevalent that Broad Creek recently has become part of Oprah Winfrey's O Ambassador Program; last year, the students raised money to build a school in eastern Asia.

Cathy's commitment to meet the systemic needs of her teachers has done wonders for teacher retention rates; teachers at Broad Creek often stay "way beyond" the age when they are eligible to retire. Last year, 25 percent of the teachers could have retired but asked to stay and continue working. "As long as it's still fun," Cathy explained, "they want to come to work. But, as a leadership team, we sit down with them and say, 'We want you to continue teaching, but you have to be open to change.' We thought that getting that buy-in from the veteran teachers would be a high hurdle, but they have embraced it." Furthermore, of the 44 teachers currently on staff, only seven have less than five years of teaching experience.

> By listening to and believing in her staff, and by looking outside of education to find out what works, Cathy Tomon has shaped Broad Creek Middle School into a place where teachers and students love to be. She refuses to let the waves hold her back.
>
> *Source:* C. Tomon, principal, Broad Creek Middle School, personal communication, September 1, 2009.

ENGAGE FAMILIES AND THE COMMUNITY IN A MEANINGFUL AND GENUINE WAY

Part of creating a positive and collaborative working environment within a school is being sure to engage all stakeholders that have an impact on teachers' working lives. The list of these stakeholders clearly includes those who are in the building every day, such as administrators, students, and other teachers, but it should extend outside the building as well and into the community. The frequent call to bridge the communication gap between school-level professionals and community members speaks to the breadth of that gap in current times (De Carvalho, 2000). Research is clear that teacher mobility is higher in schools and districts where community and parent involvement is lower, and low community involvement is correlated with higher levels of poverty and crime (Allensworth, Ponisciak, & Mazzeo, 2009). However, just because these factors are correlated in the research does not indicate that they must go hand-in-hand; schools can open their doors to families in a meaningful way regardless of the demographics of their students. In some places, school administrators have been very thoughtful about reaching out to parents and community members (see the vignette on Freedom Elementary School).

Setting the Community Table

Engaging All Support Structures at Freedom Elementary School

As an at-risk school in academic emergency, Freedom Elementary School was poised for change. Open to engaging community partners and out-of-school support systems, the school became a site for twenty-first-century after-school support and, after seeing positive results from this support, the school was given the opportunity to become a pilot site for community-school matching under the Ohio Community Collaboration Model for School Improvement (OCCMSI). As an intervention model, OCCMSI helps schools to integrate contextual supports with traditional school-improvement reforms, operating within the belief that once a school succeeds in fostering positive change in the nonacademic components of school (such as youth development and health services), the academic components will soar. As former principal Jean Snyder explained, "We were doing all this work on the intervention side for academics, but nobody ever really worked with us on the behavioral side." Under her leadership, Freedom Elementary won an OCCMSI grant, and the work began.

The first step toward OCCMSI implementation was to develop Community Table, a forum for the leaders of the school to sit down with teachers, students, parents, and community-based organizations to strategize about systemic reforms that could help Freedom out of its slump. To begin, the school became a direct partner with the Children and Family First Council in its district, which gave Jean and her faculty a figurative seat at the table with "all of the major nonprofits in the area," including the school, United Way, Boy Scouts and Girl Scouts of America, area mental health agencies, and many others. After fostering a relationship with the Council, many members of this governing body became stakeholders at Freedom's Community Table. Taking a proactive approach to the OCCMSI model of reform, the Community Table members developed a list of the top five nonacademic barriers to student success, deciding that they would begin their intervention from there. The list included the following issues:

1. Lack of parent engagement
2. Lack of physical health services
3. Lack of behavioral mental health services
4. Truancy
5. Stress on faculty members due to the pressure to make adequate yearly progress (AYP)

After forming this list, Jean began to think strategically about surrounding herself, her staff, and her students with all supports available. She engaged members of the Community Table to come up with out-of-school youth development activities to mirror the positive learning experiences the students were having while at school. She wrote a grant to the state department for an Access to Better Care Initiative, which housed health and therapy services under the roof of Freedom.

The results were swift and impressive. Freedom Elementary School went from being the school in the district with the highest number of latecomers to the lowest; the attendance rate soared to 95 percent. With the wraparound services involved and the student participation rates so high, much of the stress indicated from barrier number five was eliminated. As Jean said, "We were feeling pretty good about ourselves." It seems that the OCCMSI theory was correct—once Freedom was able to engage parents and community partners, the school went from academic emergency to continuous improvement in one year. The following year, Freedom achieved adequate yearly progress, and last year Freedom was named an Effective School under AYP. Principal Snyder explained that students have a significantly more difficult time focusing on improving their studies when they have weighty out-of-school worries. Once there are solutions in place to alleviate these concerns, however, academic achievement becomes much more attainable.

Many of these solutions were catalyzed at the Community Table and involved the engagement of nonprofit organizations and health-services providers. It is also essential, Jean pointed out, to get parents and caretakers on board. The teachers at Freedom had to make a real commitment to inviting parents into their classrooms, both to share in the successes of their children and to collaborate on solving problems.

Teachers also had to be willing to listen to the needs of those parents, just as Jean had listened to the teachers' requests. When parents asked for increased one-on-one communication with teachers, for example, Jean set up a system of exit and entrance conferences that involved teachers, parents, and students and gave the children an opportunity to showcase their own growth (as evidenced through data collection). These conferences helped parents to understand why enriching summer programs are important for their students as well. Overwhelmingly, reported Jean, the teachers were in favor of opening their doors. When asked if any of her faculty members were hesitant about this initiative, she explained, "When your tent's on fire, you get everybody on board pretty quickly. If you're in academic emergency, your tent's on fire, and you don't have a lot of time to fix it. So you get everybody's attention at a much different level."

With all pistons firing, Freedom Elementary School is on its way to being a model of student success and community partnership. "We're all in the same business," said Jean. "That Community Table surrounds us."

Source: J. Snyder, former principal, Freedom Elementary School. personal communication, September 10, 2009.

ENSURE THAT TEACHER WORKLOADS ARE REASONABLE

One of the selling points for a more robust parent and community outreach strategy is that it relieves some of the burden on teachers to bear primary responsibility for those children's education. Parent involvement in promoting student learning helps to ensure that teacher workloads are reasonable. In short, reasonable workloads promote effective instruction by creating time for teachers to properly plan, prepare, and reflect. By hiring a sufficient number of teachers and other school support personnel, teachers can focus on their most important task: engaging learners and increasing student achievement. Furthermore, by assigning teachers only to subjects in which they are fully proficient academically and, at a minimum, highly qualified as defined under the No Child Left Behind Act, school-level leaders and administrators can keep their teachers satisfied and effective (Johnson, Berg, & Donaldson, 2005).

Another potential benefit of promoting regular communication between parents and teachers is increased agreement on behavior management and discipline issues. When a student acts out in class, it is much easier for a teacher to decide on and implement action steps if she can reach out to that student's parents or guardians for clues that may inform the cause of the behavioral misstep. In a recent study conducted by Learning Point Associates and Public Agenda, nearly 70 percent of teachers surveyed rated the removal of students with severe behavioral problems as a "very effective" strategy for promoting teacher effectiveness (Coggshall, Ott, & Lasagna, 2010). Similarly, the role of school leadership in mitigating some of the burden on teachers to address frequent offenders allows teachers more time to focus on instruction and improves the classroom environment so that time spent on learning is maximized.

Comprehensive Change for Increased Results

The Teacher Advancement Program in Columbus
Chief Academic Officer Marvenia Bosley believed in the promise of professional learning communities as a way to promote high levels of teacher collaboration that could lead to other school-level reforms. Five years ago,

with three reconstituted schools on her hands, she was looking for a way to engage the students and teachers at those schools in a thoughtful and innovative way. Bosley's initial strategy was to partner with The Ohio State University to initiate some sort of teacher-learning academies where "other teachers from other schools could go and have job-embedded professional development, and learn, and then go back to their schools." Although the program showed some promise, the results were not as impressive as the district had hoped. At this point, Bosley approached Columbus Education Association President Rhonda Johnson about turning the learning academies into Teacher Advancement Program (TAP) schools. With the Ohio Department of Education already showing interest in Columbus being a TAP site, all Bosley needed was the consent of Johnson and her union leaders. When asked to reflect on her first response to this proposal, Johnson said simply: "You know, instead of saying what you're against all the time, I believe in saying what you're for. We're *for* improving student achievement. We're *for* trying something new and not saying no to it." Four schools in the district—the three learning academy schools and one additional school—began their pre-TAP year immediately.

TAP is a four-pronged reform model. Each TAP site includes the following elements:

- Multiple career paths for teachers
- Ongoing applied professional development for teachers
- Instruction-focused accountability
- Performance-based compensation

President Johnson pointed to the two components that, in her opinion, have made the strongest impact on their schools. First, the differentiated career ladder has provided many new opportunities for teachers to take on leadership roles. The TAP model features master and mentor teachers in each school; these expanded practitioner roles allow teachers to coach and mentor their colleagues while still spending some time in the classroom. This new career ladder also provides an easy segue into some form of differentiated compensation.

Even better than the differentiated career paths, Johnson argues, is the "cluster group" system of professional learning. As the "ultimate professional development opportunity," the cluster groups are beneficial because "teachers work together to develop a strategy, go off into their classroom to test the strategy, and then analyze student work to evaluate the strategy" (in TAP language, this action plan is call "field testing").

These strategies, when taken together, are like a toolbox of methods and lessons to help students become critical thinkers. As the field-test agents, the teachers are helping foster their own critical thinking skills as well.

The structure of differentiated pay in Columbus has two main components: expanded salaries for master and mentor teachers and bonuses for student achievement. The master and mentor teachers operate using a regular teaching contract and a supplemental contract that pays the stipend in one lump sum at the end of the year. As far as performance bonuses go, there are both schoolwide awards and, in the elementary schools only, individual awards based on growth. Using value-added measures, the district determines the overall academic growth of students in a given TAP school. If the school shows over one year of growth, every teacher receives a bonus. In the elementary schools, if a teacher shows over one year of growth for his or her respective students, he or she can also receive an award.

As teacher advocates, union leaders are often in favor of differentiated career ladders and job-embedded professional development and learning. What, though, was Johnson's take on the performance-pay aspect of TAP? Was she concerned that the individual awards would become a perverse incentive for teachers, encouraging them only to "cheat" their way to higher test scores? Was she concerned that once the teachers were "competing" against one another for increased salaries, all trust among the faculties would be lost? Quite the contrary. When asked about her feelings on whether using value-added measures was the best way to determine the allocation of performance awards, Johnson replied, "I think it's the fairest way. It's much better than just a score on an achievement test, because what we're really working on is student growth. We've been pushing for a growth model for a long time, so I'm glad we use value-added as opposed to just a test score." In fact, President Johnson believed so strongly in the TAP program that when the Ohio Department of Education was awarded a Teacher Incentive Fund grant, she stated that she would sign on to the use of the funds only if they were utilized to expand their current TAP model.

President Johnson will tell you in no uncertain terms that, as a school improvement model, TAP works. She points to her high-poverty, at-risk urban schools in particular, saying that these schools that had always struggled in the past made AYP the first year of TAP implementation; the urban high school is just "a few points away" from being an Effective School. As a union leader, she acknowledges that teacher buy-in is necessary in a system such as TAP, and for this reason expanding TAP to every school in a district would be impossible. On the other hand, she noted: "There's nothing wrong with trying something new. When it's not punitive, when it's substantial enough that it makes a difference, when it's legally defensible, why not try it? I know there's no research out there that says that something like [TAP] works, but these programs are all new. The salary schedule *can* change, and we've seen that work effectively."

Source: R. Johnson, president, Columbus Education Association, personal communication, September 3, 2009.

ENSURE THAT SCHOOLS ARE SAFE, CLEAN, AND APPROPRIATELY EQUIPPED FOR EFFECTIVE TEACHING

The literature on the distribution of highly qualified, effective teachers shows that they tend to move away from large, urban schools populated by at-risk, minority youth (Imazeki & Goe, 2009). One of the reasons for this mobility is that these schools often lack the resources needed to ensure positive, clean, and safe conditions for their faculties. When asked to report on the top-ranking factors that influence their decisions about where to work, teachers rate facilities, class size, and access to resources higher than student performance or socioeconomic status (Allensworth, Ponisciak, & Mazzeo, 2009). Because the quality of facilities and access to resources are highly correlated with these student demographics, however, the outcome is that too often teachers stay away from schools with poor facilities and poor students.

Poor and unsafe school conditions such as polluted air and poor ventilation can lead to decreased student achievement due to health hazards. In the 2006 report *Building Minds, Minding Buildings,* the American Federation of Teachers (AFT) notes that, "schools, students, and teachers are being held accountable for improved academic performance, but the task is extremely difficult in subpar buildings" (p. 5). In the same report, AFT staff writers list the following key elements for school leaders to consider when attempting to create a "well-designed, well-built, well-maintained school" (p. 9):

- *Proper siting, taking into account the environmental impact*
- *Building and classroom sizes that are conducive to learning*

- *Design appropriate to climate and region*
- *Adequate ventilation, heating, and air conditioning systems*
- *Extensive use of natural daylight*
- *Acoustic materials that reduce noise levels that interfere with learning*
- *Safety and security concerns effectively addressed*
- *Technology that is integrated into academic and building design*
- *An infrastructure that supports special needs students and adults*
- *Adequate staffing to keep schools clean and well-maintained (p. 9)*

As a school leader, then, it is critical to consider the physical attributes of a school that contribute to a safe and comfortable workplace. In addition, school leaders must consider the human capital involved in creating positive working conditions, such as students, parents, and the teachers themselves. School-building conditions can greatly influence teachers' ability to teach, and they send a message about the value of school and learning overall. By guaranteeing a safe school and ensuring that teachers feel valued, respected, and comfortable in their place of business, principals can promote a culture that has educators and students alike wanting to work hard (Johnson, 2006). We recognize that this is no easy feat, particularly in a place with limited support from the local community. However, district leaders in Clark County, Nevada, were not daunted by the lack of community engagement and began a proactive campaign to convince the private sector that their support to improve the working conditions in schools would attract new teaching talent to the community, which would in turn result in a more educated local workforce, providing a long-term return on their initial investment!

"Put Your Money into Teachers"

Empowerment Schools in Clark County, Nevada
The education-minded business leaders of Las Vegas, Nevada, saw an opportunity. Several of the schools in the Clark County School District were in need—in need of financial resources, guidance, and a plan. These

leaders dipped into their toolkit of turnaround models within the business community and began to craft a framework for a new school design that would increase student achievement and accountability. The business-community members convened a Central Design Team featuring, other than themselves, members of the school board, Clark County district officials, parents, and teachers. Empowerment Schools were born.

Three years ago, in the first stage of implementation, four elementary schools in the district were chosen for Empowerment: Kirk Adams, Lee Antonello, Paul E. Culley, and Rose Warren. In speaking with George Ullom, assistant principal at Paul E. Culley Elementary School, he mentioned that the schools were chosen for different reasons and that Culley in particular was chosen because it was low performing but salvageable, due to demographics, leadership capacity, and several other factors. He explained: "It's not like taking a school that has been in Needs Improvement for five years and trying to reformulate it. Culley had only been in Needs Improvement for one year and wasn't a school in need of reconstitution. [District officials] didn't want to send the message that only those low schools were eligible or worthy."

In design, admits Principal Ullom, the empowerment model looks a lot like a system of site-based management, although he pointed out that there is much more to it than that. Qualities particular to the Empowerment Schools in Clark County include the following:

- Extra funding to be used at the discretion of each school's administration
- The autonomy to change the school calendar
- The authority to create a new union contract for empowerment teachers (originally a memorandum of understanding)

In short, each of the Empowerment Schools has been allowed to "tweak what education looks like at a school." For Paul E. Culley, this has translated into an increased attention to and creativity around two facets: teachers and time. With the extra money allocated to their school, the principals of Culley have chosen to fund an extra full-time teaching position and extend the teacher work calendar by twenty-nine minutes per day and five days per year. This extension is the equivalent of each teacher receiving a 9.6 percent bonus. Principal Ullom cites this raise in salary as an attractive incentive for teachers to come to Culley and stay.

When asked to speak to the low attrition rates at Paul E. Culley and to elaborate on the ways in which the empowerment model has affected them, Principal Ullom explained: "Money doesn't make people better or happier workers, but it keeps them in the building. We're a Title I school in a poor economic area. Typically, at an old inner-city school, the kids come a little rough around the edges, and it's harder to keep staff; they come, and they work, and they move on. On our staff, though, we have a lot of veterans. Our staff is not leaving." Teachers not only are showing their support with their feet but also are rating the elementary school high on the annual Teaching and Learning Conditions Survey, which serves as a barometer of teacher perceptions of working conditions in Clark County.

So the money helps. The other essential empowerment factor at Paul E. Culley that serves to significantly increase teacher support and job enjoyment is the faculty's role in school governance. Every school in the system is required by law to have a School Empowerment Team (SET), a governing body that consists of one representative from each of the following stakeholder groups: administration, support staff, faculty, teachers' union, and parents.

At Paul E. Culley, Principal Ullom and former principal Lisa Primas decided that if teachers were going to take ownership over the governance of the school, the SET would need to expand to include more of their voices. The SET now includes a representative from every department and each grade level in the school. The team votes on every major decision that takes place at the school, from instructional and curriculum decisions to choices about changing the school calendar, budget and staffing, and governance. To help inform decisions, before each SET meeting representatives from the team convene meetings of their respective grade levels or departments to gather input on the topics that will be discussed. This expansion, said Principal Ullom, has helped to promote fairness and equity and to grow trust at Paul E. Culley in a major way. "No big school decisions are made without teacher votes. Nothing that happens here is just the principals' decision; in fact, we've been overridden by the SET in the past, and we've always abided by the SET's decision. At Culley, teachers know that the SET is not just a sham." This level of buy-in, George believes, is key to morale. More so than even strength of leadership, the empowerment model's incorporation of teacher input is an integral and crucial component to increased practitioner satisfaction and, ultimately, performance.

Although Principal Ullom champions the success of the empowerment model at Paul E. Culley, he also acknowledges that it is not for everyone. In light of this reality, and to allay some of the union's initial fears about implementing such a model, the teachers' contract for Empowerment Schools has an opt-out component: if at any time a teacher feels that working within the conditions of an Empowerment School is not for him or her, he or she can opt out, and the district will find that teacher another job in the district. On the other hand, a school itself is not allowed to opt out" a teacher by force instead, the school must counsel and coach that individual, providing more targeted professional development and mentoring. In this way, then, even the staffing is in the best interest of the faculty.

The Empowerment School model in Clark County, Nevada, is the story of a business community's commitment to its children. The Empowerment School model at Paul E. Culley Elementary School is the story of an administration's commitment to its teachers.

Source: G. Ullom, personal communication, September 11, 2009.

Taken as a comprehensive set of ingredients, working conditions in a school can be a powerful tool. When school leaders think strategically about maximizing the quality of working conditions in toto, levels of teacher retention and job satisfaction should begin to rise. Important conditions to consider include, but are not limited to, engaging family and community members, cleaning up the physical conditions of the school building, and promoting a school culture that allows teachers to collaborate, adequately plan, and feel both respected and useful. Principals who approach these conditions as a system, rather than attempting to deal with each one individually, will see the best results for both their faculty members and their students. The rubric that follows is intended to help administrators make connections between investments in better working conditions and other aspects of the educator talent management system.

Rubric 1.1. Is Your Plan for Providing Positive Working Conditions for Teachers Connected to and Complemented by the Other Key Educator Talent Management Areas?

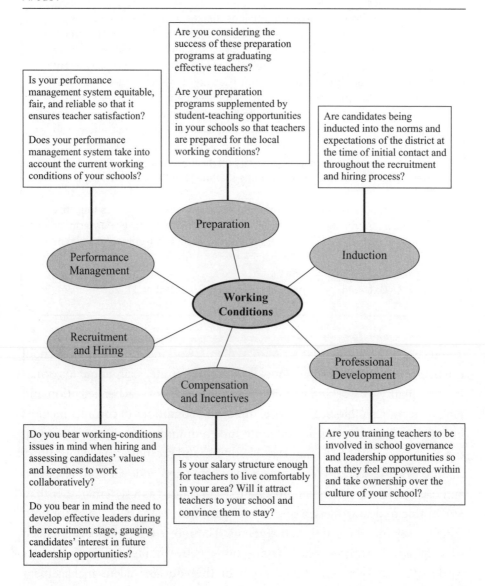

Are you considering the success of these preparation programs at graduating effective teachers?

Are your preparation programs supplemented by student-teaching opportunities in your schools so that teachers are prepared for the local working conditions?

Is your performance management system equitable, fair, and reliable so that it ensures teacher satisfaction?

Does your performance management system take into account the current working conditions of your schools?

Are candidates being inducted into the norms and expectations of the district at the time of initial contact and throughout the recruitment and hiring process?

Preparation

Performance Management

Induction

Working Conditions

Recruitment and Hiring

Professional Development

Compensation and Incentives

Do you bear working-conditions issues in mind when hiring and assessing candidates' values and keenness to work collaboratively?

Do you bear in mind the need to develop effective leaders during the recruitment stage, gauging candidates' interest in future leadership opportunities?

Is your salary structure enough for teachers to live comfortably in your area? Will it attract teachers to your school and convince them to stay?

Are you training teachers to be involved in school governance and leadership opportunities so that they feel empowered within and take ownership over the culture of your school?

WORKING CONDITIONS CHECKLIST

	Yes	No	N/A
1. Does your school have a positive, collaborative, team-oriented culture that facilitates effective teaching?	☐	☐	☐
Do you ensure that there is common planning time to allow for teacher collaboration?	☐	☐	☐
Do you actively foster a professional and trusting school atmosphere?	☐	☐	☐
Do you work to ensure that the curriculum is neither over- nor underprescribed, so that teachers enjoy both direction and autonomy?	☐	☐	☐
2. Does your school effectively maintain discipline?	☐	☐	☐
Do you help equip teachers to apply best practices in classroom management?	☐	☐	☐
Do you work to create class sizes that are small enough for teachers to effectively deal with discipline problems?	☐	☐	☐
Do you provide teachers with consistent support when it comes to administering disciplinary policies?	☐	☐	☐
3. Are your school facilities safe, clean, and appropriately equipped for teaching?	☐	☐	☐
Do you quickly repair any unsafe school structures?	☐	☐	☐
Do you oversee the upkeep of the school grounds to ensure that teachers feel respected and comfortable in their physical work environment?	☐	☐	☐
Do you keep a pulse on whether teachers believe they have sufficient classroom instructional resources to teach effectively?	☐	☐	☐
4. Does your school maintain reasonable workloads for teachers?	☐	☐	☐
Do you work with others to make sure a sufficient number of staff are hired to keep class sizes reasonable?	☐	☐	☐
Do you see to it that teachers are assigned only to classes in which they are fully proficient academically?	☐	☐	☐
Do you engage in interest-based bargaining over workload and staffing protocols?	☐	☐	☐

From Their Schools to Yours: Getting the Ball Rolling

1. Cathy Tomon began to think strategically about working conditions at her school after reading the results of the North Carolina Working Conditions Survey. Identify similar initiatives in your own state that would serve as an entrée into reform.

2. Jean Snyder was committed to incorporating her school's community into her efforts to improve working conditions for her teachers. Think about the resources that your school's community has to offer. How can you tap into these resources to enrich the experience of both your teachers and your students?

3. The implementation of Teacher Advancement Program (TAP) schools in Columbus, Ohio, has helped school and union leaders think about working conditions systemically. How would a comprehensive reform agenda such as TAP be implemented in your school? What policy levers would need to be in place for this to happen? What issues might you face? What impact might it have?

4. In Clark County, Nevada, the Empowerment Schools model involves teachers in school-level policymaking in an authentic way. How are teachers engaged in governance at your school? How could they become more involved? What could be done to give faculty a sense of ownership? How would a sense of ownership help with faculty support and buy-in?

REFERENCES

Allensworth, E., Ponisciak, S., & Mazzeo, C. (2009). *The schools teachers leave: Teacher mobility in Chicago Public Schools.* Chicago: Consortium on Chicago School Research.

American Federation of Teachers (2000). *Building a profession: Strengthening teacher preparation and induction.* Washington, DC: Author.

American Federation of Teachers (2006). *Building minds, minding buildings: Turning crumbling schools into environments of learning.* Washington, DC: Author.

Coggshall, J., Ott, A., Behrstock, E., & Lasagna, M. (2009). *Supporting teacher effectiveness: The view from Generation Y.* Naperville, IL: Learning Point Associates.

Coggshall, J., Ott, A., & Lasagna, M. (2010). *Convergence and contradictions in teachers' perceptions of policy reform ideas.* Naperville, IL: Learning Point Associates.

De Carvalho, M. (2000). *Rethinking family-school relations: A critique of parental involvement in schooling.* Mahwah, NJ: Erlbaum.

Fine, S. (2009, August 9). Why I left teaching behind. *The Washington Post*, p. 1.

Gimbel, P. A. (2003). *Solutions for promoting principal-teacher trust.* Lanham, MD: Scarecrow Education.

Imazeki, J., & Goe, L. (2009). *The distribution of highly qualified, experienced teachers: Challenges and opportunities.* Washington, DC: National Comprehensive Center for Teacher Quality.

Johnson, S. M. (2006). *The workplace matters: Teacher quality, retention, and effectiveness.* Washington, DC: National Education Association.

Johnson, S. M., Berg, J. H., & Donaldson, M. L. (2005). *Who stays in teaching and why: A review of the literature on teacher retention.* Cambridge, MA: Harvard Graduate School of Education, Project on the Next Generation of Teachers. Retrieved September 15, 2009, from http://assets.aarp.org/www.aarp.org_/articles/NRTA/Harvard_report.pdf

North Carolina's Teacher Working Conditions Initiative (2008). *North Carolina's Teacher Working Conditions Initiative.* Retrieved December 2, 2009, from http://northcarolinatwc.org.

CHAPTER TWO

Getting the Right People on the Bus

How School Districts Manage Teacher Recruitment, Hiring, and Placement

Applications are flowing in. You should feel relieved, knowing that dozens, even hundreds, of candidates are interested in your posted vacancies, but instead you continue to feel uneasy. There are more resumes than you can review for your social studies, English, and art positions, yet not enough in other subjects, and even less interest in the positions at the highest-need schools in the district. Plus, none of the applications stand out as exceptional. How can you make your schools exceptional if you cannot find teachers to hire who seem committed to go above and beyond in their drive to excel? What would such a teacher even look like in the hiring process? How, you wonder, can you and your colleagues at the district and school buildings work together to really reform your recruitment and hiring process and make hiring exceptional teachers for all students a reality?

OVERVIEW

The previous chapter described the crucial role of school principals in ensuring the type of school climate that encourages retention of more highly effective teachers. But school leaders alone cannot accomplish the type of systemwide advancements that are needed. To significantly improve teacher quality, they must work together with the range of other stakeholders, and especially with school districts. This chapter will focus on district-level activities and how you can help to foster collaborative reform between school- and district-level leaders. School districts play a role in each of the eight key teacher-quality policy areas: preparation, recruitment, hiring, induction, professional development, compensation, working conditions, and performance management. With the exception of teacher preparation, the district role is significant in each of these areas that affect what takes place in school buildings. More than any other role, districts most directly and significantly influence teacher recruitment and hiring.

Districts attend recruitment fairs and post advertisements to reach out to potential applicants. They coordinate the collection and screening of applications—and in some cases they select teacher candidates. Districts advertise themselves and the profession to teachers and at the same time decide which individuals will join the ranks of veteran teachers influencing children's lives every day.

As Jim Collins explains in *Good to Great,* "getting the right people on the bus" and in the right seats is a necessary prerequisite to successfully planning a route to improving performance (Collins, 2001). With the right people on board, schools can effectively adapt their course as and when circumstances require. With the wrong people on the bus, no improvement strategy, however well designed, can fully realize its intended effects.

Even though school districts vary immensely—with New York City schools serving nearly one million students, compared with rural districts that may serve fewer than two hundred students—all school districts share the common goal of securing excellent teachers who can deliver the district's mission and equip all students with the type of education that will help them succeed in an increasingly complex marketplace and society. The extent to which teacher quality policies and practice are determined at the district level versus the school building level varies, with a tendency for principals in smaller districts to take on responsibilities that district administrators or human resource departments in larger districts often adopt.

In leading teacher recruitment and hiring, districts increasingly collaborate with schools. For example, in most districts principals lead the interview process (Liu & Johnson, 2006). More and more often schools are the primary players in the hiring process (Plecki, Alejano, Knapp, & Lochmiller, 2006). For example, in Chicago and Seattle, teacher candidates apply directly to schools, limiting the district's role to a more administrative one.

But in most, if not all, cases, the first several steps in the hiring process take place at the district level. These steps include projecting vacancies, marketing the positions, launching the application process, and prescreening candidates. Subsequent steps can be taken at the district or school level. These steps include more detailed screening, such as interviewing; observing lessons; reviewing writing samples, resumes, and other application materials; and, finally, selecting the strongest candidate. However, even for the initial steps that are coordinated by the district, school leaders may be involved to varying degrees. For example, principals can and should play a role in helping districts to project vacancies through creating a collaborative work environment and encouraging teachers to give early notice of any departure plans. In addition, principals and other school leaders can attend job fairs to meet candidates and speak specifically about their schools and any vacancies. Finally, in highly decentralized systems, principals can lead the prescreening of candidates.

As a school or district leader, you are a member of the stakeholder group ultimately responsible for systemwide employment decisions, and you must accommodate the diversity of opinions in the field about what constitutes an "ideal" teaching candidate and what types of strategies will attract candidates who fit this description. The characteristics of the "ideal" teaching candidate, as well as the strategies that will lead to their recruitment, vary by geographic, demographic, and social settings. But in leading the critical task of recruiting teachers, districts should follow these four general guidelines:

1. Hire the best possible candidates.
2. Distribute teachers appropriately and equitably across schools and classrooms.

3. If the pool of excellent teacher applicants seems too shallow to hire excellent teachers for all students, work to widen the pool.

4. If outstanding applicants are not accepting your offers, take a comprehensive look at your educator talent management system and work to address deficiencies.

HIRE THE BEST POSSIBLE CANDIDATES

When it comes to teacher recruitment and hiring, you know that there is no room for complacency—every teacher must be highly competent, caring, and capable of teaching each and every child. This is not only because teachers are the most important school-level factor when it comes to improving student learning, but also because the effect of high-quality teachers is cumulative. Students assigned to a more highly effective teacher for three years in a row performed as much as forty-nine percentile points higher than students assigned to a less effective teacher (Jordan, Mendro, & Weerasinghe, 1997). Therefore, districts must assist schools in recruiting and hiring not just *some* excellent teachers but *only* excellent teachers.

Although the primary motivation for recruiting and hiring effective teachers is, of course, to improve student learning, there is also a financial benefit to making the right decisions about this human resource function. For one, replacement costs related to teacher turnover that results from poor teacher-school matches at the time of hiring are expensive. In addition, the recruitment and hiring stage is also critical because the costs of removing teachers who turn out to be ineffective can be exorbitant. For example, in New York state during the 1990s, the average cost of dismissing a teacher was estimated at $200,000 (Kahlenberg, 2006, p. 18). The attorney's fees associated with dismissing a teacher alone costs a district more than $100,000, with overall costs in some cases exceeding $400,000 (Hess & West, 2006, p. 31). Districts must assist schools in understanding the appropriate steps to take to terminate ineffective teachers and to do so in a cost-effective way. But, more important, they should endeavor to hire teachers for whom this issue will not arise.

One talent management expert in the private sector explained the centrality of the hiring decision, writing: "If you have only one dollar to spend on either improving the way you develop people or improving your selection and hiring process, pick the latter. . . . Hiring for the right skills is more efficient than developing those skills" (Wellins, Smith, & Erker, 2009, p. 8). Wellins et al. (2009) support this approach for the following reasons:

- A strong match between employee and employer is critical to preventing high turnover, and it is much more difficult to change the organization's work or culture than to hire individuals whose skills and interests are appropriate for the job.

- Some critical skills, such as judgment and adaptability, often cannot be easily developed.

- Even for skills that can be developed, assessing whether candidates have them at the time of hire is more cost-efficient than trying to develop them later.

But how can a hiring committee determine who the right people are, when teaching is such a multifaceted activity? The 41st Annual Phi Delta Kappa/ Gallup Poll of public opinion on education found that the public's views of what made for a high-quality teacher in 2009 differed quite dramatically from their views twenty-five years ago (Bushaw & McNee, 2009). Whereas the ability to communicate, relate, maintain discipline, and be patient were at the top of the list of desired attributes twenty-five years ago, qualities such as being caring, enthusiastic, intelligent, and committed to teaching are valued today (Bushaw & McNee, 2009). When the goals of an education system are so varied and complex, identifying the right hiring criteria is not an easy task. Furthermore, how do hiring committees differentiate the good candidates from the great?

The Highly Qualified Teacher definition established in the No Child Left Behind Act is recognized as merely a minimum standard (Honawar, 2008). These criteria stipulate that each classroom be staffed by teachers who are fully certified, have at least a bachelor's degree, and demonstrate subject mastery in the class taught. Recently, the national debate has turned from teacher qualifications to teacher effectiveness, with federal funding through the American Recovery and Reinvestment Act (ARRA) prioritizing efforts to improve teacher effectiveness and teacher distribution among four overall improvement priority areas.

However, your job is made challenging by the fact that no criteria for an "effective teacher" can capture the innumerable demographic, professional, and personal characteristics that differentiate teachers from one another. It goes without saying that candidates should be assessed for their likely effectiveness in the classroom—but also hiring committees should be directed to consider the balance between creating a diverse staff and a like-minded group of educators who can successfully work together. Questions to ask may include:

- In order to provide students role models who are "like them," is there sufficient diversity in terms of teachers' race and gender? In terms of teaching tolerance and breaking down prejudices, is there a sufficient number of teachers who differ from the majority student population in these regards?

- In terms of teaching philosophies, are staff members sufficiently like-minded to implement a cohesive curriculum, while maintaining enough diversity of philosophy for meaningful dialogue about challenging the status quo in improving the curriculum?

- In terms of teachers' professional backgrounds, is there a good mix of experience in the classroom, rich pedagogical expertise, and practical experience from other professions that career changers are able to bring real-life lessons into the classroom?

Achieving a balance between homogeneity and diversity in your teaching staff has implications for the extent of decentralization in hiring arrangements that you wish to employ. On the one hand, decentralized, or school-based, hiring can benefit equitable distribution because individuals who are on site are better able to hire candidates who will "fit" within the school atmosphere and thus be more likely to succeed and to stay.

On the other hand, decentralized hiring may negatively affect equitable teacher distribution if the poorer-performing schools in effect "select" less effective teachers. For example, research has found that different principals value different types of teacher characteristics, and an individual principal's unique views on the characteristics of an effective teacher are reflected in his or her teacher hiring decisions (Rutledge, Harris, Thompson, & Ingle, 2008). In theory, this could result in the possibility that ineffective school leaders hire ineffective teachers. At the very least, districts must carefully screen all applicants at the district level for quality and provide oversight to guarantee that students are not shortchanged as a result of a decentralized hiring process.

Recruiting Teachers in Vancouver School District, Washington

In 1997, the Vancouver School District (VSD) realized that 80 percent of its 1,300 teachers were eligible to retire within five years. At the same time, the school board was intensively engaged in transforming the district's approach to instruction to one that was more collaborative and team-based and focused more on differentiating instruction for every individual child. The impending wave of retirement became a window of opportunity to recruit effective teachers who could put these changes into action.

Before recommending any reform, Lee Goeke, the district's new human resource (HR) director, conducted research on HR management in public education and the effectiveness of each HR process and its potential for reform. Armed with data and well-thought-through ideas, the newly professionalized HR department reached out to the various stakeholder groups—the school board, the principals, and the teachers' union—to begin reforms, and largely gained their support. The first reform was the development of complementary competency models for teachers and for school leaders. These competencies were embraced by the leaders and teachers who helped develop them. This move directly affected the district's recruitment and retention system, because school leaders who understood, embraced, and personified the new competency model were able to interview prospective teachers and convey the changing model for teaching and learning and demonstrate the strong school leadership support they would receive.

A recruitment strategy was developed that strove to recruit 25 percent of new teachers from within the district and local community, 20 percent from elsewhere in the state, 20 percent from elsewhere in the

Pacific Northwest region, and 35 percent from elsewhere in the United States or abroad. But what really allowed them to hire the best candidates was the implementation of values-based hiring. It was believed that you can teach pedagogy, but you cannot teach values. Values such as commitment to children learning, belief in the value and richness of diversity, willingness to be held accountable, and ability to generate excitement in the classroom so that children were motivated to learn were assessed during the screening process, and candidates were selected accordingly.

Following these recruitment reforms, the district saw measurable increases in teacher quality and retention and student achievement, and decreases in teacher performance problems and disciplinary incidents. By the time 65 percent of the teachers had been replaced, the district had a cumulative five-year retention rate exceeding 90 percent and a corresponding 80 percent decrease in performance and discipline issues. More recently, similar reforms have been replicated in other districts with similar success, demonstrating the universal benefits of a values-based model.

Source: L. Goeke, former associate superintendent of human resources management, Vancouver School District, personal communication, August 12, 2009.

School districts have come a long way since the last century in advancing their processes for hiring the best candidates. In the past, school district hiring practices often included criteria that would be seen as highly inappropriate today. As an example, in the nineteenth century, teacher hiring in at least one school district involved candidates' recitation of the following declarations:

> *I promise to abstain from dancing, immodest dressing, and any other conduct unbecoming a teacher and a lady.*
>
> *I promise not to go out with any young man except as it may be necessary to stimulate Sunday-school work.*
>
> *I promise not to fall in love, to become engaged, or secretly married.*
>
> *I promise to sleep eight hours a night, eat carefully, and to take every precaution to keep in the best of health and spirits, in order that I may be better able to render efficient service to my pupils [Minihan, 1927, p. 606].*

Although school districts have advanced significantly to meet the needs of a twentieth-century education system, it is clear that there remains much room for improvement if districts are to advance the education system for the twenty-first century and beyond.

DISTRIBUTE TEACHERS APPROPRIATELY AND EQUITABLY ACROSS SCHOOLS AND CLASSROOMS

One aspect of teacher recruiting and hiring that especially needs district attention is the distribution of teachers among high-poverty, low-performing schools and low-poverty, high-performing schools. In addition, researchers and policymakers alike accept the fact that shortages of teachers are never a universal problem but rather an issue specific to certain subjects and geographic areas (Ingersoll, 2003; Ingersoll & Perda, 2009). The burden of this problem of uneven distribution falls disproportionately on children who come from poor and minority backgrounds (Imazeki & Goe, 2009).

Inequitable distribution, referred to by former U.S. Secretary of Education Margaret Spellings as education's "dirty little secret," can take place between regions, districts, schools, and classrooms (Imazeki & Goe, 2009). District-level action, namely through more effective recruitment and hiring, is viewed as a key component for rectifying teacher distribution problems.

School-level leaders, especially principals in at-risk schools, play a critical role in improving teacher distribution, as outlined in Behrstock and Clifford (2009). Specifically, school leaders greatly affect the working conditions in a school, including those aspects of working conditions that most centrally affect teachers' decisions about where to work—student behavior and parental engagement. As discussed earlier, they also play a role in teacher hiring and can affect teacher distribution at this stage. School leaders in high-need areas should be encouraged by districts and other leaders to:

- Actively represent the school in a positive and accurate light to applicants, particularly with regard to the aspects of working conditions that are most positive.

- Develop partnerships, both formal and informal, with colleges, universities, districts, and other principals to more efficiently target effective novice teachers who might consider teaching at their school.

- Hire effectively, if principals are involved in the hiring process, by emphasizing teacher *effectiveness* (for example, leading to improved student outcomes) more than teacher *qualifications* and taking into account candidates' ability and willingness to commit to teach in a high-need environment.

- Assign teachers in a way that will help new teachers to acculturate to the school environment (for example, mentors and coteaching opportunities) and to focus their time on developing their practice (for example, assigning limited administrative duties) so that they can be effective.

In addition to working with school leaders to improve teacher recruitment and achieve a more equitable distribution of teachers, districts should work with teachers' unions toward this end. In many cases collective bargaining agreements hinder the equitable distribution of teachers by forcing principals to consider teachers transferring from within the district before other candidates, but in some cases teachers' unions also have been found to work toward creating a better distribution of teachers. By surveying several dozen collective bargaining agreements in Florida, Cohen-Vogel and Osborne-Lampkin (2007) find that contracts are often more lenient about teacher assignments than you may think and that principals often assign teachers in an unequitable manner not because of union-imposed barriers, but rather because of ingrained norms and pressure from some teachers and parents to keep the most effective teachers in the most well-off areas.

The importance of teacher distribution was highlighted at the national level in the No Child Left Behind Act and further confirmed as a federal priority in the 2009 American Recovery and Reinvestment Act. ARRA includes four assurances for the receipt of federal funds, with one including the goal of improving teacher effectiveness and the equitable distribution of teachers. Clearly, recruiting and hiring for equitable teacher distribution is a concern across the full spectrum of teacher-quality stakeholder groups. However, districts take the lead in achieving this widespread priority.

Although attracting and retaining teachers in certain high-need settings depends on a whole host of factors—many of which can be difficult to change in the short-term—following are some immediate and research-supported strategies that you might consider in order to achieve a more equitable distribution of teachers:

Focus on improved school security and student behavior. Research shows that teacher attrition away from high-need schools is greater in settings where student discipline is problematic (Allensworth, Ponisciak, & Mazzeo, 2009). The following two resources can help you improve security and student behavior:

1. *Safe and Orderly Schools.* The American Federation of Teachers developed this guide to facilitate the creation of more safe and orderly environments (see http://www.aft.org/pubs-reports/downloads/teachers/safeandorderly4pgr.pdf).

2. *School Safety and Security Toolkit.* The National Crime Prevention Council has developed a step-by-step guide for parents, schools, and communities to work together to improve school safety (http://www.ncpc.org/cms-upload/ncpc/File/BSSToolkit_Complete.pdf).

Improve parental involvement. In a recent survey of Generation Y teachers, Public Agenda and Learning Point Associates found that, when asked which single change would improve the teaching profession, 23 percent of respondents cited better parental involvement, accountability, support, and communication. This was the highest rated response, with twice as many teachers citing it over any other single change to the profession. Following are two resources available to help you facilitate better parental engagement:

1. *Critical Issue: Supporting Ways Parents and Families Can Become Involved in Schools.* Developed by Learning Point Associates, these audio clips and other resources present strategies straight from the mouths of experts (see http://www.ncrel.org/sdrs/areas/issues/envrnmnt/famncomm/pa100.htm and http://www.ncrel.org/sdrs/areas/issues/envrnmnt/famncomm/pa300.htm).

2. *Ninety-Two Ways to Involve Families and Communities in Education.* The Hawaii and Iowa Departments of Education provide additional information to help schools engage families and communities in education (http://www.k12.hi.us/~konawahs/92_ways_to_involve_families.htm and http://www.iowaparents.org/files/involvingparentmshstch.pdf).

IF THE POOL OF EXCELLENT APPLICANTS IS TOO SHALLOW, WORK TO WIDEN THE POOL

Research on teacher recruitment and hiring identifies a number of concrete strategies that districts should consider to widen the pool of excellent teachers. Following are some short-term, medium-term, and long-term possibilities for your consideration:

Short-term strategy: implement early hiring timelines. Although not without some hurdles to be overcome, one straightforward, easily implementable, highly important way to improve the pool of teacher candidates is to hire early. The bulk of your hiring should take place from February through May, not May through August, for example. A 2003 report by The New Teacher Project (TNTP), a nonprofit group dedicated to closing the achievement gap by securing high-quality teachers for all students, discovered that many school districts lose the opportunity to hire highly credentialed teachers because they begin the hiring process too late in the school year, and they give their current faculty the opportunity to fill new vacancies first before opening up the process to new candidates. According to researchers Levin and Quinn (2003), the candidates that are lost from the pool as a result of late hiring timelines tend to be the most highly qualified candidates. In order to implement an earlier hiring timeline, districts should do the following:

- Require exiting teachers to give vacancy notifications early
- Align hiring timelines with district recruitment efforts
- Ensure that transfers within the district occur early
- When possible in light of tax revenue projections, produce earlier and more predictable budgets

- Generate accurate and early enrollment estimates (Levin & Quinn, 2003; Liu & Johnson, 2006)

Medium-term strategy: promote, increase, and market the characteristics of the district that attract teachers. Every district has its selling points, be they related to compensation, working conditions, leadership, or the community. As a medium-term strategy for increasing the size of the pool of excellent applicants, districts should identify these marketable attributes and then work to advertise these at recruitment fairs and in other venues with the potential to reach individuals who might consider applying to the district (Guarino, Santibanez, & Daley, 2006; Hayes & Behrstock, 2009).

These efforts to promote teaching in your district can extend far beyond small-scale word of mouth and include more formal district promotion. Districts or consortia of districts within a region may create public relations, advertising, and marketing departments that use technology and other media to promote teaching in their schools. Or districts may initiate a full-fledged advertising campaign, as did the New York City Public Schools (Hayes & Behrstock, 2009). See the sidebar in this section for more information on this campaign.

The New Teacher Project recommends widening the teaching pool by targeting recruitment strategies for particular types of shortage-area teachers, based on the factors that often motivate people from particular backgrounds to

---

Widening the Teaching Pool in New York City Public Schools

The New York City Department of Education (NYCDOE) I Teach NYC campaign was launched to widen the pool of high-quality teachers for the city's high-need schools. The ad campaign includes advertisements on subway cars, busses, bus stop shelters, billboards, television, and a web site (www.teachNYC.net) where prospective teachers can view videos of current New York City public school teachers and principals, as well as school chancellor Joel Klein, talking about the profession and the city's schools. Their advertisements can be viewed at www.adcouncil.org/default.aspx?id=244.

As an additional strategy to widen the candidate pool, the NYCDOE also promotes its New York City Teaching Fellows program, an alternative certification route to teaching, through advertisements on subway cars, busses, bus stop shelters, billboards, television, and a web site (www.nycteachingfellows.org).

teach. For example, special education teachers, whose interest in teaching often stems from experience with someone close to them who has special needs, might be more receptive to recruitment strategies based on personal interactions and referrals. Strategies to recruit teachers in this shortage area, therefore, should involve such personal outreach (Daly, 2009).

By contrast, mathematics and science professionals who are interested in teaching are motivated by the desire to teach a subject that fascinates them (Daly, 2009). They use the Internet more than any other group. Strategies to recruit mathematics and science teachers should therefore include online outreach and should emphasize the content areas that these professionals can teach. Finally, minority teachers are often drawn to the profession by the desire to address inequalities and give back to a community that may reflect the group they are in (Daly, 2009). Strategies to expand the pool of minority teachers should therefore draw attention to these aspects of teaching.

Long-term strategy: develop relationships with all potential applicant pools. Like most districts, you probably already have relationships with *some* potential applicant pools, but over the long term districts that need to expand their applicant pool to provide an excellent teacher for every student should develop relationships with *all* potential applicant pools (Ingersoll & Perda, 2009; Spradlin & Prendergast, 2006). Specifically, relationships should be cultivated with these groups:

Maximizing Community Resources to Enrich the Teaching Pool

In 2008 the federal government gave ten awards to school districts and community-based organizations for the Full Service Community Schools Program. Each initiative involved creating multisector partnerships that would engage an entire neighborhood or community in a transformative shift of schooling. This policy decision reflects the need to think about moving the concept of "school" out of the brick-and-mortar classroom and into the larger community. And as this conversation gains momentum, several promising models for this kind of inclusive involvement are springing up.

The nationwide Citizen Schools program, for example, operates a national network of apprenticeship programs for middle school students, connecting adult volunteers to young people in hands-on learning projects after school. The program works particularly hard to connect local scientists and engineers with public school students. Recently the model was selected by *Time* magazine as number three on the list of Twenty-One Ways to Save America.

- Teacher education programs, both traditional and alternative, and undergraduate, graduate, and community colleges

- The reserve pool of teachers, including retired teachers

- Paraprofessionals or active community members who cannot typically afford to undergo formal teacher training, but could be recruited through Grow-Your-Own or other alternative programs

- High school students whose interest in teaching as a career may be sparked by future educator or other such programs

- Overseas agencies that can expand the pool of foreign language exchange teachers, such as native Spanish or Chinese speakers

- Community members with special skills and knowledge who may not *become* teachers, but who may complement the work of teachers as engaging guest speakers on relevant topics

Strategies in Tough Economic Times

Although tough economic times often lead to state and district budget cuts and consequent short-term district layoffs or reduction of force, the silver lining in some instances is the opportunity to reassess whether the existing talent pool matches current district learning priorities. In addition, declining prospects outside of teaching naturally widen the pool of people desiring careers in teaching, as those previously on the fence lean increasingly toward the schoolhouse. But they also create additional responsibilities for those hiring teachers to ensure that there is agreement on the greatest recruitment needs in a district and that the hiring criteria reflect those needs and are well understood by everyone involved.

In addition, some new recruits may be treating teaching as a "fallback" career, so hiring committees must screen especially carefully to weed out candidates who are joining the profession for the wrong reasons. Therefore, it is important that you take steps to increase the rigor of the screening and interview processes to ensure that teacher candidates enjoy working with young people, meet state qualifications to teach, demonstrate strong classroom management skills, and are committed to helping all students learn (see Rubric 3.1).

Strategies for Overcoming Special Challenges

Teacher recruitment is one of the most important educator talent management functions for all districts, but certain types of schools and districts present specific challenges. In the following sections, the teacher recruitment challenge is elaborated for the contexts of urban schools, rural schools, and schools with large populations of English language learners.

Urban Challenges

When it comes to teacher recruitment, large urban school districts often suffer from the bureaucratic inefficiencies that can prevail at large public institutions. Without effective leadership and communication, the varied efforts across the district to improve teacher recruitment do not result in a coherent or effective recruitment program. When real or perceived challenges with student discipline and motivation are also present, the result is that many talented teachers accept positions in less high-need suburbs where working conditions are more manageable.

The New Teacher Project found that in fact roughly 80 percent of teachers prefer large urban districts to low-need ones, but that late hiring timelines and other bureaucratic problems cause them to accept positions in other districts (Levin & Quinn, 2003). These problems are relatively straightforward to fix. Some urban districts have partnered with TNTP to address these issues and recruit more effective teachers, including Baltimore, Chicago, Denver, Memphis, New Orleans, New York, Oakland, Philadelphia, and Washington, D.C. Through TNTP alone, these districts have recruited more than 37,000 new teachers, affecting 5.9 million students (The New Teacher Project, 2010).

Rural Challenges

Even though recruiting teachers to rural areas is not universally problematic, there are certain poor "hard-to-staff rural schools" that continually face recruitment challenges (Monk, 2007). The roots of these recruitment problems differ, of course, so their solutions must differ as well. For example, in contrast with urban areas, there are few problems with student discipline in these rural schools, but instead problems with the lack of local amenities to afford teachers the quality of life they might be used to elsewhere. Improvements in the availability of telecommunications and computing services therefore may greatly benefit such districts (Monk, 2007).

Administrators in rural districts should also bear in mind that even though the cost of living in rural areas tends to be comparatively low, there are additional hidden costs of teaching in hard-to-staff rural areas. Because of the lack of public transportation, suitable housing, and other services, teachers may be required to spend more than they otherwise would on automobile, home ownership, and other expenses. The following questions can guide leaders in rural areas seeking to address such recruitment problems:

1. Have you attempted in the past to recruit teachers from other regions to your rural area?

   a. If so, what strategies have you found to be most successful? Can these be replicated and expanded?

   b. If not, what barriers prevented you in the past from reaching out to potential teachers outside of your immediate geographic area?

   c. What factors would dissuade teachers from other areas to move to your rural area? Can these issues be addressed or counteracted by emphasizing the positive attributes of your area?

2. Have you attempted to recruit teachers from other professions within your region?

   a. If so, who have you reached out to? Paraprofessionals in schools? Active community members? Career changers looking to make an impact?

   b. Why would those in your region who chose other professions do so over teaching? Are the drawbacks to teaching real or perceived? Can they be reversed?

After determining whether it is best to reach out to teachers outside the area or to nonteachers within the area, you should then take the same approach as nonrural districts in determining the mix of incentives that are most likely to attract such individuals to your schools.

English Language Learners

With 10 percent of students now English language learners (ELL), the demand for teachers of this persistent shortage subject is high. Moreover, nearly half of all teachers in the United States have at least one ELL in their classroom (Zehler, Fleischman, Hopstock, Stephenson, Pendzick, & Sapru, 2003). Because of the large number of ELLs and the diversity of languages they may speak, recruiting teachers who can help them learn is a challenge in some areas. The first step for districts is to project the number and types of ELL teachers that they will need. Even this straightforward step, however, can be difficult in many rural areas, where large numbers of migrant workers' children are ELLs. When actively recruiting ELL teachers, districts should look for candidates who not only speak the necessary languages but also understand the cultural background of the ELL students in the school. Then the district should train non-ELL teachers in working effectively with these new recruits.

Twenty-First-Century Teacher Recruitment in the Rural Arkansas Delta Region

Some districts can rely on newspaper, radio, and other advertisements to recruit the teachers that they need. But in certain high-need small towns in the rural Delta Region of Arkansas, such local papers and radio stations do not even exist, let alone produce results for teacher recruitment. Technological and other agricultural developments have led to the loss of workers and communities in this farmland, draining the region of potential teachers for the children who do remain.

Beverly Williams, the assistant commissioner for human resources and licensure at the Arkansas Department of Education (DOE), explained, "The number-one problem is housing. Young people must live thirty minutes away from where the schools are located in order to find housing, a life, a community."

To reverse this dire situation, twelve hard-to-staff districts are participating in a pilot program with the Arkansas DOE that involves developing targeted recruitment strategies and training staff to recruit teachers. Known as the Delta Pilot Initiative, this effort got under way in January 2010. Among its features are:

- The placement of teacher recruitment billboards in higher-traffic areas
- Assistance with purchasing recruitment material (such as display boards, folders, and flash drives with the district's application)
- Reimbursement by the DOE of district recruitment advertising costs
- Coordination of job fairs and job fair displays, to give a professional, cutting-edge face to these districts
- An opportunity for districts to come together to learn from each other's successful recruitment efforts

In addition, they have solicited the help of the national online teacher recruitment portal (www.teachers-teachers.com) to assist them in designing attractive recruitment web sites.

Alongside the Delta Pilot Initiative, the DOE has been encouraging talented individuals at all stages of the career development continuum to join and strengthen the teaching profession. For the younger generation, the Teachers of Tomorrow program provides a trainer in each district involved with the program to spur the interest of students in the teaching profession by creating clubs, providing mentoring and tutoring to develop skills, and allowing older students to serve as classroom assistants to teachers.

Department of Education Teacher Recruitment Program Advisor Camille Sterrett said, "It's important to start early because students decide by eleventh and twelfth grade what they want to be as adults and if they want to go to college or not." In the case of older individuals, the DOE has, among other initiatives, encouraged district Grow-Your-Own initiatives to solicit the interest of talented professionals already invested in the community, including school paraprofessionals and career changers, to become licensed teachers.

To address the housing issue head-on, the state has developed laws to incentivize the redevelopment of old downtown neighborhoods, including the building of apartment complexes and the provision of financial assistance with home ownership in these parts of the state.

Because the Delta Pilot Initiative does not exist in a vacuum, isolating the effects of this project is challenging, although the preliminary outcomes hold promise. "The number of applications to teacher preparation programs has increased," said Sterrett, "although it still is too early to tell the outcome of this initiative."

Source: B. Williams, assistant commissioner, Arkansas Department of Education, and C. Sterrett, teacher recruitment program adviser, Arkansas Department of Education, personal communications, February 18, 2010.

IF OUTSTANDING APPLICANTS ARE NOT ACCEPTING YOUR OFFERS, REVIEW YOUR EDUCATOR TALENT MANAGEMENT SYSTEM

This chapter has suggested that the districts' role in recruiting the best teachers, effectively distributing them across schools and classrooms, and, where necessary, widening the pool of applicants are pivotal for successfully improving teacher quality. What, then, if a district is trying to do each of these things, but top applicants continually accept competing job offers, or new hires persistently leave the district within several years of their employment?

In these cases, school districts need to comprehensively review each of their educator talent management functions and strategically make improvements that will make working in the district more gratifying to excellent teachers. Figure I.2 in the Introduction illustrates the connections between teacher recruitment and these other policy components, demonstrating how recruitment is tied to nearly every other type of teacher-quality reform. Recruitment is closely linked with salaries, opportunities for professional development, and, in particular, working conditions, because it is far easier to recruit excellent teachers when these workplace characteristics are appealing. Most important to new teachers choosing where to teach is the existence of supportive school leadership (Milanowski, Longwell-Grice, Saffold, Jones, Schomisch, & Odden, 2009).

TeachNOLA

On August 29, 2005, Hurricane Katrina struck New Orleans, devastating the city. The hurricane was the costliest in America's history, leaving thousands of residents displaced. The deep teacher shortage that resulted was just one of many pressing problems the city faced as it tried to pull itself back together. In spite of this mass destruction and competition for resources and support, The New Teacher Project (TNTP) and the Recovery School District of Louisiana formed a partnership to ensure that the city's need for effective teachers would not be ignored in this time of turmoil. Together with New Schools for New Orleans, a nonprofit organization dedicated to excellent public schools, they created teachNOLA, a recruitment initiative designed to ensure that the city's schools could hire excellent teachers.

In the months that followed the hurricane, teachNOLA developed a comprehensive and strategic approach to recruiting high-quality teachers locally and nationally. It's clear that New Orleans benefited from the widespread interest in helping to rebuild the city. But more important, teachNOLA was able to recruit hundreds of talented teachers through aggressive outreach and a streamlined application process.

For example, teachNOLA quickly posted a web site and e-mail address and made a commitment to provide excellent customer service by dealing efficiently and professionally with all potential applicants. Initial inquiries received a response within two days. Qualified candidates received invitations to interview within two weeks of submitting an application and information on the interview's outcome within another two weeks. In addition, interviewees were allowed to sign up online for their interview time and date.

This quick response time is critical. TNTP's research in urban districts has shown that delayed hiring and poor communications with applicants hamper teacher hiring. In one urban district in the Northeast United States, for example, TNTP found that more than half of teacher applicants never even received a response from the district, costing the district high-quality candidates.

According to teachNOLA's Ana Menezes, who previously managed and now oversees the program, "TeachNOLA makes sure that no piece of the application process is overwhelming to applicants, and no aspect of applying serves as a barrier." Such streamlined, aggressive recruitment enables the program to build a large pool of quality applicants. It uses a three-stage selection process to choose the best among them. In 2009, just 7.5

percent of applicants were invited to join teachNOLA—an acceptance rate typical of the nation's top universities.

Because many recruits are in transition—be it from city to city or from one career to another—teachNOLA's focus on customer service helps to ease what can be a stressful time. A *Moving Guide* is available to help with those new to the area, and staff are prepared to answer questions about neighborhoods and local amenities. From the earliest stages, candidates are given opportunities to interact with the district's schoolchildren, allowing the aspiring teachers to see their potential impact on students and building excitement for what the experience will hold. TeachNOLA sends a clear message early on that its goal is to raise student achievement in schools where children have lagged behind for too long.

TNTP and the Recovery School District recognize that an effective recruitment strategy extends beyond adopting a number of best practices such as the preceding. It requires the support and involvement of various stakeholder groups across various points on the teacher career continuum. In New Orleans, the quality of the preparation that new teachers receive is considered a vital part of their success in the classroom. TeachNOLA teachers are prepared through an intensive preservice Training Institute that is embedded in the city's schools. Once they successfully finish the institute and begin teaching, they complete TNTP's Louisiana Practitioner Teacher Program (LPTP), an innovative pathway to certification. LPTP is designed specifically to prepare career changers and recent graduates to raise student achievement in struggling schools. In recent studies, the program's graduates have been found to perform better in mathematics and reading instruction than teachers, including experienced teachers, certified by other programs.

The success of teachNOLA's recruitment efforts also depended in part on the Louisiana Department of Education's support for such alternative route preparation programs. The department oversees regular collection of value-added data on the effectiveness of the teachers who graduate from the state's preparation programs, so that the Recovery School District and districts across the state can be confident that new teachers emerging from this program will be equipped to teach effectively.

Moving from the state to the school level, teachNOLA also actively works to involve school leaders. Said Menezes, "We really try to involve school principals in every decision that we make." Principals are invited to speak at events, kept in the loop on program recruitment, and asked for candidate referrals from their pool of paraprofessionals and other nonteacher educators. Especially during the hiring season, coordination with school leaders is seen as a key element of a successful recruitment strategy. "By always centering conversations around our shared goals of providing great teachers for all students, we are able to work effectively with multiple stakeholder groups," said Menezes.

The results of these recruitment efforts are highly promising. Today, 91 percent of all public schools in New Orleans have a teachNOLA teacher on staff. Of school principals with these teachers, 100 percent report that teachNOLA has had a positive effect on student learning. The program has drawn 7,600 applications to date and brought 420 teachers to high-poverty schools. In 2009, 105 teachNOLA teachers took positions in struggling schools. Of new teachers entering classrooms through the program in 2009, 79 percent teach in high-need subject areas like mathematics and science.

For a recruitment initiative to ultimately be effective, those who are recruited must also be retained over time. A key strategy of teachNOLA is to consistently present throughout the application process the same clear mission to recruits: every classroom in the city deserves to have an effective teacher who is totally focused on raising student achievement. By being clear at the recruitment stage about this mission, they are more likely to attract candidates who are equally committed to the same goals and thus are more likely to commit to remaining in the profession over the long run. Across TNTP's teacher recruitment initiatives, 87 percent of teachers start a second year, and 75 percent start a third year—higher than national averages for new teachers working in urban schools.

For more information about the teachNOLA initiative, visit www.teachnola.org.

Source: A. Menezes, site manager, The New Teacher Project/TeachNOLA, personal communication, January 27, 2010.

Districts can most effectively address these salary, professional development, working conditions, and other educator talent management policies to improve recruitment by working together with other stakeholder groups, such as teachers' unions, school principals, and local boards of education. Other factors being equal, compensation plays a part in individuals' choices of employment. Even though salary is not the driving motivation behind people's decisions to teach, it is still often a consideration at the margins—when deciding which district to teach in and whether to join and remain in the teaching profession at all. Teacher salaries comprise 60 to 80 percent of a district's budget on average (Barber & Mourshed, 2007). Therefore, if the compensation package offered to top teacher candidates is not sufficiently attractive, there may be little room left in the budget to provide additional financial incentives. Increasingly, districts are beginning to review their compensation programs and engage the unions in dialogue to modify the structures of teacher pay scales so that they are especially attractive to teachers who bring about significant improvements in student learning (see www.cecr.ed.gov for examples).

Second, opportunities for ongoing professional growth are important to all workers, and especially to teachers, who clearly value learning yet sometimes worry about the stagnation that may result from teaching the same material year after year. Teachers' professional development should be ongoing, job-embedded, and of high quality (National Staff Development Council, 2001). But more often, it consists of one-off workshops that are disconnected from teachers' everyday work. One aspect of ongoing, job-embedded professional development is high-quality induction that clearly lays out professional expectations of teachers and includes mentoring by experienced, effective teachers who can help to advance new teachers' instructional practice from their first day on the job. Districts should work with school leaders to create high-quality induction programs to aid teachers' immediate growth and development when they need it the most. Finally, high-quality working conditions are consistently identified by teachers as a key factor in their decisions to go to or leave a school.

Once a district is satisfied that its educator talent management system is strong, it should ensure that teacher applicants are aware of how an aligned set of human resource functions affects them professionally. An information-rich hiring system should be developed, so that prospective employees are able to learn about the district before accepting an offer (Liu & Johnson, 2006). The rubric that follows is intended to help districts determine which aspects of their educator talent management system are aiding recruitment and hiring, and which aspects may be detrimental to recruiting the best teachers for all students in the district.

Rubric 2.1. Is Your Plan for Recruiting and Hiring Effective Teachers Connected to and Complemented by the Other Key Educator Talent Management Areas?

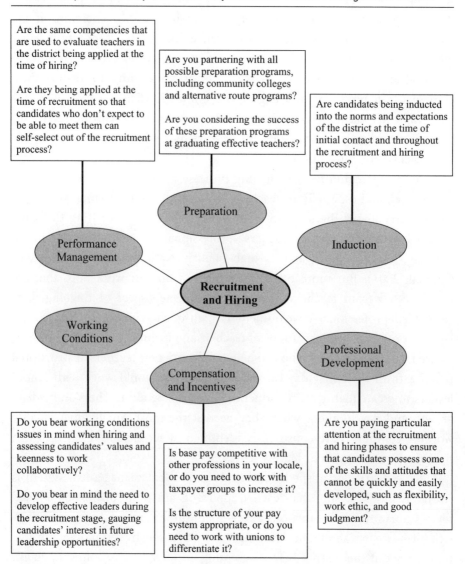

Are the same competencies that are used to evaluate teachers in the district being applied at the time of hiring?

Are they being applied at the time of recruitment so that candidates who don't expect to be able to meet them can self-select out of the recruitment process?

Are you partnering with all possible preparation programs, including community colleges and alternative route programs?

Are you considering the success of these preparation programs at graduating effective teachers?

Are candidates being inducted into the norms and expectations of the district at the time of initial contact and throughout the recruitment and hiring process?

Preparation

Induction

Performance Management

Recruitment and Hiring

Working Conditions

Professional Development

Compensation and Incentives

Do you bear working conditions issues in mind when hiring and assessing candidates' values and keenness to work collaboratively?

Do you bear in mind the need to develop effective leaders during the recruitment stage, gauging candidates' interest in future leadership opportunities?

Is base pay competitive with other professions in your locale, or do you need to work with taxpayer groups to increase it?

Is the structure of your pay system appropriate, or do you need to work with unions to differentiate it?

Are you paying particular attention at the recruitment and hiring phases to ensure that candidates possess some of the skills and attitudes that cannot be quickly and easily developed, such as flexibility, work ethic, and good judgment?

RECRUITMENT AND HIRING

	Yes	No	N/A
1. Does your district promote, increase, and market the characteristics that are attractive to teachers?	☐	☐	☐
Have you identified these draws of the district?	☐	☐	☐
Have you worked to strategically advertise these draws throughout the recruitment process?	☐	☐	☐
2. Does your district set a high, unyielding standard for teacher quality when identifying and selecting candidates?	☐	☐	☐
Do you set recruitment and retention goals and track how well you meet them?	☐	☐	☐
Do you pay particular attention to ensuring that students from high-need backgrounds are not taught by teachers of a lower standard?	☐	☐	☐
3. Does your district have or actively develop relationships with all applicant pools?	☐	☐	☐
Do you partner with both traditional and alternative teacher preparation programs to recruit their graduates?	☐	☐	☐
Do you reach out to the reserve pool of former teachers, including retirees?	☐	☐	☐
Do you cultivate future teacher talent by encouraging paraprofessionals, teacher aides, high school students, and others to consider becoming a teacher?	☐	☐	☐

TEACHER RECRUITMENT CHECKLISTS

Suppose your district identified the following priorities for hiring new teachers: (a) recruit the right quantity of teachers; (b) recruit the right quality of teachers; (c) place teachers in schools where they are likely to "fit" and ensure that the highest-need schools have access to excellent teachers. Suppose you then wish to use research-based strategies to achieve these priorities—where would you turn? The following steps are adapted from guidance by TNTP to ensure that the teachers they recruit are likely to be successful (Hayes & Behrstock, 2009). Does your school district do the following?

- Identify recruitment priorities at the *pre*recruitment stage, so that resources may be targeted to pools of applicants likely to be effective, retained, and capable of filling the needs of the district.

- Develop a clear list of teacher competencies based on research findings about characteristics and habits of effective teachers and adapt it for the particular positions being recruited for.

- Have a clear, standardized list of selection criteria and interview rubrics for evaluating candidates.

- Train principals, HR staff, and all those involved with teacher selection to effectively apply the criteria and rubrics to eliminate bias in the recruitment process.

- Align all recruitment messages so that school and district goals and expectations are consistently communicated and inappropriate candidates opt out of the application process.

- Prioritize candidates who already have experience (with teaching, tutoring, or volunteering, for example) in the school and community environment that resembles yours, so that they know the types of attitudes, skills, and behaviors needed to be successful in this setting.

- Periodically evaluate the recruitment and selection process to see how well it succeeds in securing effective teachers.

- Use a diverse, multitiered application process that includes written responses, a teaching demo, a writing sample, a discussion session among candidates about teaching in a district like yours, and a personal interview.

REFERENCES

Allensworth, E., Ponisciak, S., & Mazzeo, C. (2009). *The schools teachers leave: Teacher mobility in Chicago Public Schools.* Chicago: Consortium on Chicago School Research.

Barber, M., & Mourshed, M. (2007). *How the world's best-performing school systems come out on top.* New York: McKinsey. Retrieved February 6, 2009, from http://www.mckinsey.com/clientservice/socialsector/resources/pdf/Worlds_School_Systems_Final.pdf.

Behrstock, E., & Clifford, M. (2009). *The equitable distribution of teachers: How school and district leaders can secure effective teachers for all students.* Washington, DC: National Comprehensive Center for Teacher Quality.

Bushaw, W. J., & McNee, J. A. (2009). Americans speak out: Are educators and policy makers listening? The 41st Annual Phi Delta Kappa/Gallup Poll of the public's attitudes toward the public schools. *Phi Delta Kappan, 91*(1), 8–23.

Cohen-Vogel, L., & Osborne-Lampkin, L. (2007). Allocating quality: Collective bargaining agreements and administrative discretion over teacher assignment. *Educational Administration Quarterly, 43*(4), 433–461.

Collins, J. (2001). *Good to great.* Retrieved August 21, 2009, from http://www.jimcollins.com/article_topics/articles/good-to-great.html.

Daly, T. (2009, May 21). *Recruiting and staffing effective teachers in tough economic times* [Webinar]. The New Teacher Project and Strategic Management of Human Capital. Retrieved January 31, 2010, from http://www.smhc-cpre.org/resources/district-reform-network/recruiting-for-effectiveness.

Guarino, C. M., Santibanez, L., & Daley, G. A. (2006). Teacher recruitment and retention: A review of the recent empirical literature. *Review of Educational Research, 76*(2), 173–208. Retrieved February 6, 2009, from http://www.aera.net/uploaded Files/Publications/Journals/Review_of_Educational_Research/7602/04_RER_Guarino.pdf.

Hayes, K., & Behrstock, E. (2009). *Teacher recruitment: Strategies for widening the teaching pool in a shrinking economy.* Washington, DC: National Comprehensive Center for Teacher Quality. Retrieved January 22, 2010, from http://www.tqsource.org/publications/RtoP_Brief_TeacherRecruitment.pdf.

Hess, F. M., & West, M. R. (2006). *A better bargain: Overhauling teacher collective bargaining for the 21st century.* Retrieved January 25, 2010, from http://www.hks.harvard.edu/pepg/PDF/Papers/BetterBargain.pdf.

Honawar, V. (2008, June 11). Teachers achieving "highly qualified" status on the rise. *Education Week.* Retrieved January 22, 2010, from http://www.edweek.org/ew/articles/2008/06/11/41hqt.h27.html?r=340508347.

Imazeki, J., & Goe, L. (2009). *The distribution of highly qualified, experienced teachers: Challenges and opportunities.* Washington, DC: National Comprehensive Center for Teacher Quality.

Ingersoll, R. M. (2003). *Is there really a teacher shortage?* Center for the Study of Teaching and Policy and the Consortium for Policy Research in Education. Retrieved January 22, 2010, from http://depts.washington.edu/ctpmail/PDFs/Shortage-RI-09–2003.pdf.

Ingersoll, R. M., & Perda, D. (2009). *The mathematics and science teacher shortage: Fact and myth.* Consortium for Policy Research in Education. Retrieved January 22, 2010, from http://www.cpre.org/images/stories/cpre_pdfs/math%20science%20shortage%20paper%20march%202009%20final.pdf.

Jordan, H., Mendro, R., & Weerasinghe, D. (1997, July). Teacher effects on longitudinal student achievement. Paper presented at the CREATE annual meeting, Indianapolis, IN.

Kahlenberg, R. D. (2006). The history of collective bargaining among teachers. In J. Hannaway & A. J. Rotherham (Eds.), *Collective bargaining in education.* Cambridge, MA: Harvard Education Press.

Levin, J., & Quinn, M. (2003). *Missed opportunities: How we keep high-quality teachers out of urban classrooms.* Washington, DC: The New Teacher Project. Retrieved February 6, 2009, from http://www.tntp.org/files/MissedOpportunities.pdf.

Liu, E., & Johnson, S. M. (2006). New teachers' experiences of hiring: Late, rushed, and information-poor. *Educational Administration Quarterly, 42*(3), 324–360.

Milanowski, A. T., Longwell-Grice, H., Saffold, F., Jones, J., Schomisch, K., & Odden, A. (2009). Recruiting new teachers to urban school districts: What incentives will work? *International Journal of Education Policy and Leadership, 4*(8), 1–13.

Minihan, T. (1927). The teacher goes job-hunting. *The Nation, 124,* 606.

Monk, D. H. (2007). Recruiting and retaining high-quality teachers in rural areas. *The Future of Children, 17*(1), 155–174.

National Staff Development Council (2001). *Standards for staff development* (Rev. ed.) [Web site]. Retrieved September 15, 2009, from http://www.nsdc.org/standards/index.cfm.

The New Teacher Project (2010). *TNTP Teaching Fellows Program.* PowerPoint presentation. New York: Author.

Plecki, M. L., Alejano, C. R., Knapp, M. S., & Lochmiller, C. R. (2006). *Allocating resources and creating incentives to improve teaching and learning.* Seattle: University of Washington Center for the Study of Teaching and Policy. Retrieved February 5, 2009, from http://depts.washington.edu/ctpmail/PDFs/Resources-Oct30.pdf.

Rutledge, S., Harris, D., Thompson, C., & Ingle, W. K. (2008). Certify, blink, hire: An examination of the process and tools of teacher screening and selection. *Leadership and Policy in Schools, 7,* 237–263.

Spradlin, T. E., & Prendergast, K. A. (2006). *Emerging trends in teacher recruitment and retention in the No Child Left Behind era* (Education Policy Brief). (ERIC Document Reproduction Service No. ED495752). Retrieved September

15, 2009, from http://eric.ed.gov/ERICDocs/data/ericdocs2sql/content_storage _01/0000019b/80/28/04/4d.pdf.

Wellins, R. S., Smith, A. B., & Erker, S. (2009). *Nine best practices for effective talent management* (White paper). Pittsburgh, PA: Development Dimensions International Press. Retrieved January 7, 2010, from http://www.ddiworld.com/ pdf/ddi_ninebestpracticetalentmanagement_wp.pdf.

Zehler, A. M., Fleischman, H. L., Hopstock, P. J., Stephenson, T. G., Pendzick, M. L., & Sapru, S. (2003). *Descriptive study of services to LEP students and LEP students with disabilities: Volume I research report.* Arlington, VA: Development Associates. Retrieved January 26, 2010, from http://onlineresources.wnylc.net/pb/ orcdocs/LARC_Resources/LEPTopics/ED/DescriptiveStudyofServicestoLEP StudentsandLEPStudentswithDisabilities.pdf.

CHAPTER THREE

The Enduring Role of Unions

Teacher Performance Management

It's that time again: the district's collective bargaining agreement is coming up for renewal. You have typically found the checklist provided by the district to assess teachers' classroom performance less than useful to inform teachers' professional growth, and lately you've been doing a lot of reading on innovative performance management and compensation systems for educators. You also know that school- and district-level administrators in neighboring districts are in conversation with their teacher associations to reform their teacher evaluation systems as part of plans to overhaul compensation. Armed with this research base and emerging examples of promising practices around the state, you are planning to pitch some contractual changes to your union leader. How will you begin the conversation?

OVERVIEW

Chapter Two discussed the crucial role that school districts play in influencing the staffing of a highly effective teaching force. Through strategies around recruitment and hiring, local school officials can begin to think systemically about getting the right people on the bus. The next question to consider is once you think you have hired the best, how can you know for sure? And how can you verify that your system for evaluating and addressing teacher effectiveness is one that encourages growth rather than one that creates extra stress or distracts teachers from doing good work in the classroom? In designing a coherent system for managing educator talent, performance management is an important mechanism for providing continuous feedback to staff. Before a district can tenure those who have been hired, consider additional compensation based on performance or differentiated responsibilities, and before school officials and teachers' associations can think about the type of professional development their teachers require, these stakeholders must put their heads together to decide on a high-quality system of performance management. In this chapter, the performance management, teacher evaluation, and compensation components included as separate pieces in the Managing Educator Talent Framework described in the Introduction of this book, are combined to make it abundantly clear how intertwined each of these components is with the others. Finally, districts are not the only stakeholders involved in addressing this component; they must collaborate with their union leaders and their principals to design and implement a system of performance management that is equitable and outcomes-based.

Teacher performance management serves two purposes: to assess competence and to foster professional development and growth. Put simply, a quality system of performance management attempts to answer the following questions:

1. What do you want to measure?

2. How do you measure it?

3. What will you do with this information?

The challenge for evaluators is to make the assessment process a meaningful experience for participants, not simply an empty exercise. An effective performance management system must be able to "distinguish great from good, good from fair, and fair from poor," and then act accordingly to retain great educators and ease chronically low performers out of the teaching profession (Weisberg, Sexton, Mulhern, & Keeling, 2009). Typically, the results of an effective evaluation have implications for these dimensions:

- Professional development and mentoring
- Staffing—including hiring, transfer policies, and leadership opportunities
- Compensation
- Working conditions—a trusting and supportive environment, for example

The rest of this chapter will discuss how effective performance management systems address the guiding questions, in addition to examples of districts and states that have begun work on these comprehensive systems. To help you get started with the design and implementation of a new approach to performance management, here are a few research-based pointers.

WHAT DO YOU WANT TO MEASURE?

The first important step is to establish a performance management system that is fair, specific, and high quality. A fair evaluation system will enable teacher buy-in and meaningful growth, as well as increase teacher morale. In order to achieve this level of fairness, the system's creators must first determine what it is they want to measure. Recently, the question of what to measure has shifted from a focus on inputs, or teacher quality, to one of outputs, or teacher effectiveness (Chait, 2009).

Research is increasingly clear that there are few direct correlations between a teacher's credentials and his or her impact on student learning (Goe & Stickler, 2008). As a result, policymakers and school officials at every level have begun to think strategically about measuring teacher effectiveness instead. In short, does it matter what a teacher is bringing to the classroom if he or she is not delivering results?

In order to measure teacher effectiveness, schools and districts should first engage a diverse set of local stakeholders to help define it. Although a definition of teacher effectiveness might include some evidence of content area knowledge and pedagogy, it should also take into account a teacher's ability to help his or her students grow and progress, both as students and as citizens. Current working definitions are multifaceted and incorporate many measures. Take, for instance, this 2007 definition offered by the National Comprehensive Center for Teacher Quality. Highly effective teachers do the following:

1. Have high expectations for all students and help students learn, as measured by value-added or alternative measures

2. Contribute to positive academic, attitudinal, and social outcomes for students such as regular attendance, on-time promotion to the next grade, on-time graduation, self-efficacy, and cooperative behavior

3. Use diverse resources to plan and structure engaging learning opportunities; monitor student progress formatively, adapting instruction as needed; and evaluate learning using multiple sources of evidence

4. Contribute to the development of classrooms and schools that value diversity and civic-mindedness

5. Collaborate with other teachers, administrators, parents, and education professionals to ensure student success, particularly the success of students with special needs and those at high risk for failure (Goe, Bell, & Little, 2008)

There are many ways to define effectiveness, but at the end of the day it must be focused on student results. And whatever variables are included in the definition, they must be predetermined and incorporated into a system of performance management if the evaluation instruments are to be well received and valid.

HOW DO YOU WANT TO MEASURE TEACHER EFFECTIVENESS?

Once school officials and union leaders have reached agreement on what good teaching is, they can design and implement the tools necessary to evaluate it. A successful system of performance management should be fair and transparent, encourage collaboration, and build trust. The following strategies can help achieve these goals.

Determine the Appropriate People to Be Involved in the Evaluation and Insure That They Are Appropriately Trained

When selecting a team of reliable evaluators for a comprehensive system of performance management, they should be just that: a team. Bringing together a group of individuals to make up your evaluation team lends validity and inter-rater reliability, as well as eliminating some of the concerns around subjectivity. The evaluators should bring both pedagogical experience and deep content knowledge to their roles. Teachers frequently report mistrust of their principals as the primary evaluator, so ensuring a broad spectrum of practitioners from experienced teacher-leaders to content experts to union representatives expands ownership and acceptance of the performance management process.

The training of the evaluation team should mimic that of your school's professional-development model, in that it should be of high quality, targeted, and results-oriented. The goal of these training sessions is to produce effective evaluators, and the design of the activities should support this goal. Including the input of both future evaluators and classroom teachers in designing the training will help to build trust and generate buy-in for the new performance-management system.

Use Valid and Reliable Evaluation Tools

From the office of the U.S. Secretary of Education to the office of a principal, the key phrase used in every description of the next generation of educator evaluation systems is "multiple measures." The old system of accountability, which relied solely on student test scores, is being phased out. Competitive opportunities to access federal funding such as the Race to the Top and the Teacher Incentive Fund call for teacher-evaluation models that incorporate several measures of effectiveness. Having more than one measure, just like having more than one evaluator, helps to ensure a fair system of performance management.

So which measures to choose? At this juncture, there is opportunity for genuine collaboration between a school district and its teacher association.

Because schools tend to be outcomes-based, they can bring to the table measures based on student growth and progress. The use of state and district standardized test scores, end-of-course exams, and portfolios of student work showcase the effectiveness of a teacher through the lens of the learners' progress. Unions, on the other hand, tend to be more input-based, so can bring measures based on teacher growth and learning to the mix. Observations, teacher portfolios, and self-assessments are examples of measures that a union might recognize as valid. With the right mix of ingredients, an evaluation recipe can consider the objectives of all stakeholders.

Although the idea of creating a comprehensive grouping of measurement instruments is innovative and new, there is no need to reinvent the wheel when determining which particular measures are appropriate for your context. Online portals such as the National Comprehensive Center for Teacher Quality's Guide to Evaluation Products can help school districts and states design a model that incorporates many different types of measures. Their web site organizes currently available teacher evaluation products into the following eight categories:

1. Classroom observations
2. Instructional artifacts
3. Portfolios
4. Teacher self-report measures
5. Student surveys
6. Value-added models
7. Student performance measures
8. Combination models

Before selecting the correct menu of options, consider taking an online assessment on your district's current approach to teacher evaluation to determine existing strengths and weaknesses (for more information on the Teacher Evaluation Scorecard, visit http://survey.learningpt.org/ScoreCard/survey.aspx?pg=1). A preassessment such as this one is helpful when you are deciding which measures will work best for your teachers, union leaders, and evaluation team. It is important to remember that the design of a brand new system relies heavily on local context.

Provide Timely and Appropriate Feedback to Teachers

It is crucial to the success of any performance-management system that the goals established at the outset relate directly to the evaluation tools designed and the evaluator training implemented. Likewise, it is necessary for the data generated through the evaluations to be translated into helpful and timely feedback for those practitioners being assessed. The loop between evaluation findings and professional development should be seamless. In this way, the evaluation system gains the respect and trust of all stakeholders involved, because rather than running the risk of seeming like a "gotcha" model, it is designed and implemented in the best interest of teachers. Rather than pointing the finger at flaws, it opens the door for improvements. Whatever classroom-based instruments your system employs to measure effectiveness, remember to include time for teachers, administrators, and evaluators to meet and discuss the results.

Work with the Union to Ensure That the Process Complies with Local Bargaining Agreements

As mentioned earlier in this chapter, the full support and trust of the local teachers association can provide endless advantages for the long-term success of any kind of education-policy reform. Instituting top-down reforms without the explicit support of the teacher associations—regardless of the strength or weakness of state collective bargaining laws—affects both program implementation and sustainability.

Because the historical mission of teachers' unions is the professional well-being of its members, union leadership is more likely to support a performance management system that focuses on teacher learning, incorporates multiple measures, and translates the results into professional-development opportunities for teachers at every level of effectiveness.

With the objectives described here in mind and the action steps in place, school and district officials can implement a system of performance management that informs teacher practice and student learning, and may be indicative of future results—allowing for more timely and targeted interventions.

WHAT WILL YOU DO WITH THIS INFORMATION?

There are considerations here for professional development opportunities, staffing decisions, and choices regarding compensation. Most important of all, the performance management system should *not* be used solely for remediation and firing. In this scenario, school officials would have to start over with new teachers after each cycle of evaluation, and this approach is not beneficial for the sustainability or climate of a successful school. Furthermore, because teachers' unions are in the business of helping current teachers perfect their craft, they will never agree to support a management structure that has levers in place to shuffle low-performing teachers out the door without any attempt to intervene and provide guidance or coaching. By instead linking performance management to professional development and mentoring, the system will result in meaningful growth for teachers and provide them with a clear, consistent message about effective practice (Taylor, 2008). Only once the link between the evaluation system and professional development is clear can a district begin forging the links between evaluation and staffing, and evaluation and compensation.

IMPLICATIONS FOR PROFESSIONAL DEVELOPMENT

Continuously assessing the quality of instruction and its impact on student learning should be the focal point for leaders at every level in a district. Assessing educator effectiveness can help districts and unions to be strategic about providing the training and mentoring that current teachers need to hone their craft. Often districts will try to use performance management to jump directly to staffing and/or compensation decisions, but this is neither productive nor cost-effective. Exiting teachers and identifying replacements are both cost- and time-intensive actions—resources that could be allocated to inform which members of your talent pool need the most support. The data generated from effective teacher evaluations can inform professional development in a targeted way, helping schools and districts to save dollars by tailoring the training to exactly what the teachers need. With multiple measures of effectiveness and varied methods of gathering information on teacher performance, an efficient professional development model will provide guidance based on genuine differences in practitioner performance. Furthermore, in order to work in harmony with teachers' unions, effective performance management should begin with a focus on support and remediation for teachers at every level in the system. once those remedies have been tried unsuccessfully within a mutually agreed-on timeline, conversations about exiting ineffective teachers from the classroom can begin.

Minneapolis Federation of Teachers 59

Rigorous Standards Equal Higher Achievement for All

In her role as president of the Minneapolis Federation of Teachers 59 (MFT 59), Lynn Nordgren has worked to advocate for her teachers by pushing for high standards of performance and appropriate compensation to match those standards. Through the years, the Minneapolis teachers' union has been amenable to entertaining innovative reform measures in the area of performance management (of which compensation is an integral component), many of which are reflected in their teacher contract. As she says, "Our union leadership makes sure that our [teacher] contract raises the quality of what we consider to be a professional."

One policy lever aimed at teacher quality and effectiveness is tenure. Nordgren explains that MFT 59 is one of the few local affiliates in the United States to specify terms for the "Achievement of Tenure" in its contract. In the Minneapolis school system, gone are the days in which teachers earn tenure merely by showing up to work three years in a row. Instead, practitioners must accomplish the following tasks before they are granted tenure:

- Know and understand all curriculum standards—both district- and state-level
- Be successfully evaluated by the principal
- Work with a teacher-mentor and an achievement tenure team closely for at least the first year of teaching
- Complete courses on nonverbal communication and peer coaching
- Acquire a certain number of professional development hours in their respective fields
- Conduct an action research project, complete with professional portfolio, and present findings to a Tenure Review Team

A teacher's successful completion of all these components of tenure achievement results in a recommendation by the Tenure Review Team to

---

rehire that individual. For those who do not immediately achieve this recommendation, there are generally two options: if that individual is right "on the line," then the team might recommend that a mentor remain with that teacher for another year, with a reevaluation process at the end. The Tenure Review Team and the union are understanding about extenuating circumstances that might lead a teacher to fail on the first try, such as being shuffled through several different jobs and therefore never really getting into a good routine. President Nordgren stresses, however, that it is not the union's policy to try to carry those who are in the wrong business. Often, if a teacher's body of work shows that he or she is in the wrong locale, content area, or the wrong profession altogether, the team will recommend not to rehire.

The standards are high for teaching quality in Minneapolis, and demonstrating attainment of these standards takes some real work. For this reason, MFT 59 feels justified in offering a promising model of differentiated teacher pay; teachers who have been vetted and show results deserve to earn more money, Nordgren explains. It became counterintuitive for teachers to be involved in such new and innovative initiatives—Achievement of Tenure and the Peer Assistance and Review Process are a few examples—but continu e to be paid according to the old salary schedule of steps and lanes. "Steps and lanes was great for its time," says Nordgren, "because it used to be that women were paid less than men, people of color were paid less than whites, elementary school teachers were paid less than high school teachers. . . . Over time, though, that schedule got convoluted . . . and eventually was not an incentive at all." The district has therefore developed a system called ProPay, which has evolved into the Alternative Teacher Professional Pay (ATPP) program. ATPP is a comprehensive compensation system that rewards teachers for dedication to their practice while also encouraging them to hone their craft. The program includes intensive professional development courses that are supplemented by teachers sharing with each other video of themselves teaching. In this way, the teachers can practice implementing their professional development coursework, coach each other on that implementation, and improve their teaching in a genuine way, while simultaneously being compensated for it.

In addition to the knowledge- and skill-based rewards offered through ATPP, differentiated bonuses are available as well. The expanded differentiated pay component of ATPP offers supplemental income to those in leadership roles, such as mentor teachers and committee members, and those willing to bolster their own education with additional master's degrees, National Board Certification, or certificates in hard-to-teach fields like ELL and special education.

ATPP has been evolving through the years, with the union leaders adding components as time goes by. President Nordgren acknowledges that positing a large-scale, comprehensive reform effort such as ATPP on teachers all at once, and from the top down, can damage trust and buy-in. "We made sure that over time we were ramping this up," she says, "but also making sure that we were communicating everything." In addition to the commitment to communication and slow, consistent change, MFT 59 leaders decided to make ATPP a voluntary system so that teachers who do not believe in performance pay or those who did not feel ready to engage at such a vigorous level could opt out. Currently, approximately 85 percent of Minneapolis teachers have signed on to the program.

Source: L. Nordgren, president, Minneapolis Federation of Teachers, personal communication, September 10, 2009.

IMPLICATIONS FOR STAFFING

When thinking about using a performance management system to inform school and district staffing, officials must expand their options past a focus on exiting ineffective teachers. Performance management can be used to differentiate staffing within a school and district, to move teachers into roles that are better suited to their interests and skill sets, and to identify teacher leaders and future mentors for new teachers. For example, a principal can establish a set of leadership positions within a school building and then use the evaluation system to identify and support moving the right people into the right jobs. Opportunities for growth—often referred to as a career ladder for teachers—can create sustainability within the teaching force by providing opportunities for highly motivated and skilled teacher-leaders to contribute to governance, mentoring, professional development, and changes in curriculum and instruction (National Comprehensive Center for Teacher Quality, 2007).

Once high-quality faculty members have been hired into the system, school officials can utilize an effective performance management system to make tenure decisions. The days of basing tenure on seniority alone are falling by the wayside; education policymakers at all levels are beginning to realize that for tenure to be meaningful, an aspect of it must be tied to performance (see the vignette on the Minneapolis Federation of Teachers 59 earlier in this chapter). When there is a sense that "working toward tenure" means more than just showing up every day, a culture of professionalism and respect is encouraged.

Plan, Do, Study, Act

Expanded Teacher Contracts in Fairfax County, Virginia

In the 2005–2006 school year, district officials in Fairfax County, Virginia, decided to revise the staffing of their schools. Given the increased awareness around positive faculty collaboration models such as professional learning communities (PLCs), the district developed a plan to foster these initiatives while simultaneously opening up differentiated staffing for its teachers. In April of that year, the county released a request for proposals (RFPs) giving principals six weeks to submit proposals for a Teacher Leadership Development grant. Within the context of the PLC culture, the proposal had to meet the following objectives:

1. Support the school's creation of a variety of innovative approaches for developing and utilizing teachers as leaders to meet the instructional needs of students

2. Strengthen the link between professional learning communities (PLCs) and student success in the Student Achievement Goals of the district: academics, life skills, and citizen development

3. Improve the efficiency, as it relates to cost and/or time, of teacher training and the general use of teachers at the school level

4. Be consistent with the tenets of professional learning communities, as outlined by Richard DuFour in his seminal work

Other than these four goals, the roles of teacher-leaders as described in the RFP were very broad, allowing each school to define the positions as they saw fit. "The only thing we wanted to ensure," explains Assistant Superintendent Leslie Butz, "was that the teacher-leaders could work to facilitate collaborative teams at their schools, so as to increase teacher and student learning." Although the specific workload of the new teacher-leaders was particular to each school, the system of contract extension was standardized. Teachers had the option to extend their contracts an extra nine days, for roughly $3,700; 14 days, for roughly $5,000; or 24 days, for roughly $10,000. The salary increase included pay and benefits.

Of the 196 schools in Fairfax County, 66 principals chose to apply for grants. After a rigorous review, Superintendent Butz awarded 22 grants to 24 schools (three elementary schools chose to join forces and combine their faculties for the PLC training). Each school was given one year to implement its particular initiative, after which there was a monitoring report. The report was meant to capture instances of teacher learning and student achievement under the new PLC model. Many themes were conveyed in the reports. A far-from-exhaustive list includes the following:

- Increased teacher collaboration and collective inquiry
- Increased use of research-based practices
- Increased teacher leadership and decision making
- Increased use of data to drive instruction
- Increased academic achievement
- Increase of appropriate professional development and training
- Increased parent involvement

The initial setup of the grants allowed for three years of funding, but after year two, Butz and her colleagues felt that some of the schools had experienced enough success that they should not have to stop. Twelve weeks into year three of the program implementation, the district decided to develop criteria for some of the schools to continue being funded as "demonstration sites." To qualify for the extension, schools were assessed on a rubric with the following items:

- Rationale
- Definition
- Implementation
- System of monitoring
- Sustainability
- Replicability

When asked to elaborate on the last component, Butz said, "We wanted schools to be able to be articulate and share, with sufficient detail, their approach, either through written documentation or program design documents or specific implementation plans, financing, all these things. Communication and the exchange of information are key aspects that the demonstration sites need to possess." After the assessment, nine schools qualified to be funded for an extra year as development sites.

Source: L. Butz, assistant superintendent of Cluster VI schools, Fairfax County Public Schools, personal communication, September 2, 2009.

IMPLICATIONS FOR COMPENSATION

Once the school and district goals for professional development and staffing have been tightly aligned to the performance management system, local education leaders can work together to consider further approaches to advancing and advocating for the teaching profession through pay. Again, the link between performance management and compensation should not be exploited to penalize, but rather to reward. Alternative compensation systems have increasingly captured the interest of policymakers in recent years because of their potential to aid with the recruitment of high-quality educators and to increase teacher retention (Springer et al., 2009).

Alternative compensation can take many forms and be directed at several different groups of teachers. Aside from the often-referenced "performance pay," alternative compensation can take the form of incentives provided for teachers working in hard-to-staff schools or hard-to-fill subject areas (such as Science, Technology, Engineering, Mathematics [STEM] or special education). There are different approaches to performance pay as well. Often, rewards will come in the form of whole-building bonuses, for raising the average achievement gains across an entire student body (Silva, 2008). Other times, bonuses can be individual, with particular teachers earning salary boosts for the positive effect they have had on their specific students (McGinley, 2009). Whether the bonuses are collective or individual, national teacher associations and their local affiliates have been very clear that bonuses can be considered only if they are tied to a reliable system of performance management.

Researchers have been hard-pressed to find a school, district, or state that is comfortable tying performance-based pay solely to standardized student test scores. This method is often deemed unfair because students enter a classroom with a host of variables that can affect their achievement, not to mention the fact that there is doubt surrounding the merit of standardized tests to assess what they are meant to assess. School systems that have begun to think creatively about tying teacher pay to student outcomes focus instead on *progress,* using growth models to track that progress throughout an entire year. In the Alaska School Performance Incentive Program (AKSPIP), for instance, the state department of education has designed and implemented a growth model to assess student achievement progress, on which administrators ultimately base compensation decisions (Cushing & Garcia, 2008). Models such as AKSPIP help teachers and administrators to evaluate a student's level of knowledge and achievement at the beginning of the year and again at the end (Cushing & Garcia, 2008).

PUTTING THE PIECES TOGETHER

It takes work to maximize the teaching quality of a school or district. There are many facets to a successful system of managing educator talent. No component of the system exists in a vacuum; there are many stakeholders and ideas that require close collaboration moving forward simultaneously at any given time. One integral component of a coherent talent development system is performance management. To launch and implement a sustainable teacher evaluation system, district and union leaders must respond to questions about measurement content and tools, as well as questions about the ultimate objectives of this measurement. A fair and equitable performance management system includes a teacher evaluation process that engages the teachers, the evaluators, and the unions. The system has the potential to facilitate quality professional development, expands a staffing chart for practitioners that allows for leadership and mentoring opportunities, and paves the way for genuine differences in teachers' performance to be identified and compensated appropriately. The impetus for such a system can be born within the central office or headquarters of the local union affiliate. Wherever it begins, though, all parties must be mission-driven and begin from a shared set of values on what is best for students as the primary outcome.

"Incentives That Make a Difference"

The NEA's Sample Salary Schedule

In the grand scheme of things, alternative compensation alone is not the answer. William (Bill) Raabe, director of collective bargaining and member advocacy for the National Education Association (NEA), explains that although rethinking the teacher salary schedule is a timely reform, it is by no means *the* answer to solving the public education crisis in the United States. "Anybody who says that all we need to do is keep the compensation

---

system the way it is, or anybody who says that all we need to do is create a brand new compensation system and everything will be fine is being far too simplistic," he says.

According to Raabe and the NEA, a revised system of teacher pay will make a difference only if tied firmly to two things: a quality professional development system and a quality teacher-evaluation system. He emphasizes the word *system* in both instances because it is his belief that although there is certainly a place for individual interventions and supports, there is also strength in numbers. Having an entire school "on the same page" with regard to professional development will help a faculty stay mission-driven and trust in each other. When asked to expand on what a comprehensive evaluation system would look like, he explained: "It should be based both on teacher inputs and student outcomes. At the same time, though, we have to be realistic about student outputs; while they are a factor, they are not the only factor. We clearly need to assess whether or not what [teachers] are doing is affecting student learning, and yet I'm not convinced that whether or not the students are learning is due to the effectiveness of the teacher. Most importantly, we have to use the evaluation system to continue to enhance, change, and improve the instruction that's going on." Ultimately, the professional development system and the evaluation system should be used to enhance, change, and improve the instruction going on within a classroom.

With these criteria in mind, Raabe and his NEA colleagues have been working to develop a sample teacher salary schedule for the future. The sample operates under these research-based assumptions:

1. A teacher should enter the profession being paid a professional-level salary of at least $40,000.

2. Once a teacher enters the profession, he or she should be able to maximize his or her salary within ten years.

3. A teacher should be able to move swiftly toward that maximum salary for gaining the knowledge and skills needed to significantly improve his or her practice.

The NEA sample is being disseminated in association with a professional development model that is teacher-vetted and linked to high-quality standards; in this case, those drafted by the National Staff Development Council. To make this link explicit, the sample schedule uses these standards to clearly define the elements within a teacher's practice that will be measured, how those measurements will be conducted, and, in the end, how pay will be attached.

As for the evaluation-system component of the sample, Raabe is less eager to say that this should be tied to compensation. Citing Richard Rothstein, Raabe explains that it is almost impossible to create an evaluation system that is not subjective. Adding pay into the mix, then, skews the validity even more. Rather, he argues, policymakers should focus first on improving the teaching of those practitioners we already have and only second on finding a way to get rid of those who do not "measure up."

Hesitant to use the political jargon of today and label the NEA's ideas as "performance pay," Raabe says it is more beneficial to the teaching profession to be explicit and transparent about the end goals of alternative compensation. He offers, "We need a starting salary that's decent, a maximum salary that's reachable, and an avenue to move to that maximum salary for both experience and the things that matter in terms of enhancing teaching practice." To this end, the NEA is clear about creating the sample schedule to help schools and districts use teacher pay to work toward the following objectives:

- Providing an outline for a career path for teachers who want to seek additional responsibility without altogether leaving the classroom
- Recognizing and rewarding teachers who attain and can demonstrate knowledge and skills that improve professional teaching
- Recognizing and rewarding improved teacher practice that is a factor in student learning and other student outcomes, based on evidence of student progress drawn from teacher documentation, student work samples, and classroom assessments
- Providing guidance on recognizing and compensating teachers for the myriad duties that their daily work entails aside from direct classroom teaching
- Positioning teachers on par with salary, professional growth opportunities, and career earnings of comparably prepared professionals

With these comprehensive objectives in place and a system of professional development and teacher evaluation on the table, Raabe and the NEA have begun to think strategically about managing the talent of their educators.

Source: W. Raabe, director of collective bargaining and member advocacy, National Education Association, personal communication, September 10, 2009.

Rubric 3.1. Is Your Plan for Performance Management Connected to and Complemented by the Other Key Educator Talent Management Areas?

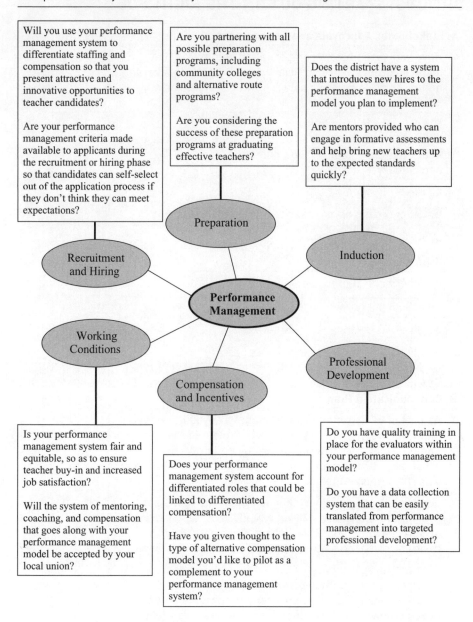

Will you use your performance management system to differentiate staffing and compensation so that you present attractive and innovative opportunities to teacher candidates?

Are your performance management criteria made available to applicants during the recruitment or hiring phase so that candidates can self-select out of the application process if they don't think they can meet expectations?

Are you partnering with all possible preparation programs, including community colleges and alternative route programs?

Are you considering the success of these preparation programs at graduating effective teachers?

Does the district have a system that introduces new hires to the performance management model you plan to implement?

Are mentors provided who can engage in formative assessments and help bring new teachers up to the expected standards quickly?

Preparation

Induction

Recruitment and Hiring

Performance Management

Working Conditions

Professional Development

Compensation and Incentives

Is your performance management system fair and equitable, so as to ensure teacher buy-in and increased job satisfaction?

Will the system of mentoring, coaching, and compensation that goes along with your performance management model be accepted by your local union?

Does your performance management system account for differentiated roles that could be linked to differentiated compensation?

Have you given thought to the type of alternative compensation model you'd like to pilot as a complement to your performance management system?

Do you have quality training in place for the evaluators within your performance management model?

Do you have a data collection system that can be easily translated from performance management into targeted professional development?

ENGAGING STAKEHOLDERS AND CONSIDERING DESIGN OPTIONS: STARTING OUT ON THE RIGHT FOOT

A. Stakeholder Approvals and Engagement	Yes	No	N/A
1. Have you assembled a compensation committee that includes school district officials as well as the teachers and/or principals whose salaries will be affected by the new plan?	☐	☐	☐
2. Have you invited the following individuals and groups to serve on the committee so that they are active participants in discussions, planning, and decisions from the beginning?			
a. Superintendent	☐	☐	☐
b. Teachers' union or association representatives	☐	☐	☐
c. Additional teachers	☐	☐	☐
d. Principal(s)	☐	☐	☐
e. Other central office personnel	☐	☐	☐
f. School board members	☐	☐	☐
g. Other community representatives	☐	☐	☐
h. State or municipal officials, if necessary	☐	☐	☐
i. Other	☐	☐	☐
B. Communication Plan	Yes	No	NA
1. As part of your communication plan, have you developed informational materials that clearly explain to teachers and principals the criteria you are using to determine which educators are eligible for a performance award and what they must do to earn one?	☐	☐	☐
2. Have you developed informational materials that clearly explain the professional development opportunities you are providing to help teachers and principals improve their performance so that they can earn a performance award?	☐	☐	☐
3. As part of your communication plan, have you developed informational materials specifically for parents that explain how the new educator compensation works and why you are implementing it?	☐	☐	☐

B. Communication Plan (*continued*)	Yes	No	NA
4. Does your communication plan include multiple means of distributing information to educators and the public (such as brochures, pamphlets, newsletters, or a web site)?	☐	☐	☐
5. At a minimum, does your communication plan include regular meetings with teachers and principals so that they can ask questions and raise concerns?	☐	☐	☐
6. Does it also provide other ways for educators to gather information quickly and easily (such as a confidential hotline, convenient after-school drop-in sessions, or trained individuals at each school site who can answer questions)?	☐	☐	☐
7. Have you developed a strategy to explain the new compensation system to the media and how awards are determined?	☐	☐	☐
8. Does your communication plan include strategies to sustain the new compensation system by building support for it among policymakers, the business community, foundations, the public, and other key stakeholders?	☐	☐	☐
C. Performance Measures	Yes	No	N/A
1. Have you decided on the method you will use to measure student achievement (such as value added or gain scores)?	☐	☐	☐
2. Have you identified the tests you will use to measure student academic performance?	☐	☐	☐
3. If you are contracting out any of the data collection and analysis, does your timeline correspond with the contractor's timeline?	☐	☐	☐
4. Have you agreed on the other sources of information you will use to assess educator performance over time? Consider the following options:			
a. Supervisors' judgments (such as principals and teacher-mentors)	☐	☐	☐
b. Peers' judgments	☐	☐	☐
c. Other	☐	☐	☐
5. Have you identified the teacher or principal evaluation instrument(s) that will be used?	☐	☐	☐
6. Have you developed a plan for training the individuals who will be using these instruments to evaluate teacher and principal performance?	☐	☐	☐

C. Performance Measures *(continued)*	Yes	No	N/A
7. Have you determined whether other teacher and administrator actions will be rewarded? Consider the following actions:			
a. Completes specific professional development activities	☐	☐	☐
b. Assumes additional roles and responsibilities (such as master teacher or teacher-mentor)	☐	☐	☐
c. Works in a hard-to-staff school	☐	☐	☐
d. Teaches a hard-to-fill subject or specialization (such as math, science, special education, or bilingual education)	☐	☐	☐
e. Other	☐	☐	☐
8. If any of the additional actions above will be rewarded, have you decided how you will weight them?	☐	☐	☐

Source: Adapted from the Center for Educator Compensation Reform, *Educator Compensation Reform Implementation Checklist*, 2007.

FROM THEIR SCHOOLS TO YOURS: GETTING THE BALL ROLLING

1. As a policy, the Minneapolis Achievement of Tenure model was the brainchild of union leaders, not school officials. Describe the relationship between the union and the administration in your district. Describe the lines of communication. What agreements could both parties make to get the conversation started?

2. In Fairfax County, district officials have differentiated the staffing options for teachers so that practitioners have more choices. What are the links between differentiated staffing and a cohort model of teaching and school governance? How might these concepts be more closely aligned?

3. According to Bill Raabe, the National Education Association supports alternative compensation, but is skeptical of tying pay to evaluation. What is the position of your union leadership on this issue? What discussions on evaluating teacher effectiveness have taken place in your district? What are the measures that you consider integral to such an evaluation system?

REFERENCES

Center for Educator Compensation Reform (2007). *Educator compensation reform implementation checklist.* Washington, DC: Author.

Chait, R. (2009). *From qualifications to results: Promoting teacher effectiveness through federal policy.* Washington, DC: Center for American Progress.

Cushing, E., & Garcia, P. (2008). *Alaska teacher and principal incentive project.* Washington, DC: Center for Educator Compensation Reform.

Goe, L., Bell, C., & Little, O. (2008). *Approaches to evaluating teacher effectiveness: A research synthesis.* Washington, DC: National Comprehensive Center for Teacher Quality.

Goe, L., & Stickler, L. (2008). *Teacher quality and student achievement: Making the most of recent research.* Washington, DC: National Comprehensive Center for Teacher Quality.

McGinley, N. (2009). *State of the school address.* Charleston, SC: Charleston County School District.

National Comprehensive Center for Teacher Quality (2007). *Key issue: Enhancing teacher leadership.* Washington, DC: Author.

Silva, E. (2008). *The Benwood plan: A lesson in comprehensive teacher reform.* Washington, DC: Education Sector.

Springer, M., Lewis, J., Podgursky, M., Ehlert, M., Gronberg, T., Hamilton, L., Jansen, D., Stecher, B., Taylor, L., Lopez, O., & Peng, A. (2009). *Texas educator excellence grant (TEEG) program: Year three evaluation report.* Nashville, TN: National Center on Performance Incentives.

Taylor, C. (2008). *Improving school performance management can improve learning.* London: Centre for Leadership and Learning.

Weisberg, D., Sexton, S., Mulhern, J., & Keeling, D. (2009). *The widget effect: Our national failure to acknowledge and act on differences in teacher effectiveness.* New York: The New Teacher Project.

CHAPTER FOUR

The View from the Statehouse

Enabling Teachers, Building the Profession

Although you have known for years that the silver bullet for improving public education is improving teacher quality, you feel disempowered and discouraged by the slow pace of change despite vowing to fight bureaucratic inefficiencies during your campaign. After an invigorating conversation with equally frustrated colleagues, you are fired up to garner the political support and willpower to lead widespread reform. You know that addressing one component of teacher quality alone will not be enough—but where should you begin in advancing a systemic approach to improving teacher quality? What approaches have other state-level players taken?

OVERVIEW

Delivering public education in the United States clearly is a multilayered and participatory undertaking, with stakeholders at every level of governance vying to give input. In the first three chapters of this book alone, the interconnections among schools, districts, local school boards, and teachers' unions have been highlighted for their potential to influence some of the key policy components that contribute to the educator's career continuum: working conditions, leadership, recruitment, compensation, and evaluation. To round out the illustration of this multilayered and coordinated system of policies and players who engage in the management and support of educator talent, the contributions of states and institutions of higher education also need to be addressed.

In this chapter, the role of state policymakers is considered, as states have a constitutional mandate to provide free and accessible public education for every child, regardless of ethnicity, language, disability, or socioeconomic status. Historically, this mandate has entailed ensuring sufficient funding for local communities to build and maintain schools where learning was presumed to take place. But state responsibilities have evolved during the past hundred years to a more robust platform of promoting equal educational opportunities through everything from certifying teachers to holding schools and districts accountable for results.

THE ROLE OF FEDERAL TEACHER QUALITY POLICY

Ensuring that every child has access to a qualified and caring teacher was a clarion call to action resulting from an exhaustive review of the research on teachers' impact on student learning conducted as part of the work of the National Commission on Teaching and America's Future in 1997. At the same time, concerns about massive pending teacher shortages (Grissmer & Kirby, 1997; National Commission on Excellence in Education, 1983) inspired states to begin to examine whether the existing teacher pipeline aligned to new state-financed reports of local supply and demand. Data on large numbers of teachers assigned to provide instruction in content areas outside their documented areas of expertise further exacerbated concerns at the state and federal levels that local communities were not allocating their teaching talent in ways that, at a minimum, promoted equal access to learning and, optimally, provided access to high levels of rigorous instruction. As reports of out-of-field teaching and the use of waivers by states to fill long-term teaching vacancies increased, the bipartisan congressional committee charged with the reauthorization of the Elementary and Secondary Education Act (ESEA) in 2001 reacted by including some of the most far-reaching federal requirements for states to ensure a high-quality teaching force.

For the first time, the ESEA included language specific to the improvement of teacher quality, and the federal law's Highly Qualified Teacher (HQT) provisions required states to report annually on the number of actively employed teachers holding at least a bachelor's degree, full state certification, and demonstration, through a variety of options, of content area mastery for the core academic subjects they taught. The ESEA focus on teacher quality was reinforced further through the 2004 reauthorization of the Individuals with Disabilities Education Act (IDEA), which introduced the requirement that all special education teachers responsible for delivering instruction in any core content area must meet HQT provisions as defined in the ESEA, while also requiring that they be fully certified to teach special education.

Given the growing pressure on states to demonstrate evidence that their teaching force meets minimum federal requirements, any doubts about whether states play a role in ensuring access to high-quality teaching talent in local communities have ceased. Increasingly, states are taking a leading role to encourage and require more robust preparation programs; more efficient human resources departments that identify, recruit, place, and support the most effective educators; and more continuous and focused support for efforts to promote and retain the best and brightest in the profession. However, as states have taken on greater responsibility for improvements in the overall teaching force due to increased federal scrutiny as well as the growth in "education governors"—who frequently raise education reform to the top of their list of policy priorities—state leaders have struggled to develop reforms that address the whole spectrum of issues that affect the effectiveness of the educator in the classroom.

Although there is growing recognition in states that improving educator effectiveness has many facets, reform efforts often are incremental in nature, disconnected from one another, and in some cases work against one another. The Introduction in this book outlines what a systemic approach to educator talent management entails and how that worldview can be applied by decision makers from the schoolhouse to the statehouse. Nevertheless, although states still struggle with focusing on the big picture, investments in policies that support teacher professional growth are on the rise—such as induction and mentoring opportunities for beginning teachers, financial incentives to pursue national recognition as an accomplished teacher through the National Board for Professional Teaching Standards, and statewide frameworks for standards of quality, research-based professional development.

BUILDING THE PROFESSION: STRONG INDUCTION AND MENTORING PROGRAMS

As teachers transition from preparation programs to the classroom, a variety of supports can make the process smoother and more effective. Perhaps chief among them is access to a high-quality induction program that includes a mentoring component as well as other forms of support, such as reduced workloads, orientation seminars, and external networks. Although induction is not universally embraced (Glazerman, Isenberg, Dolfin, Bleeker, Johnson, Grider, & Jacobus, 2010), most research has shown that it positively influences teacher retention, sense of efficacy, and actual effectiveness. Ardent proponents believe that a high-quality induction program can make or break a teacher during his or her initial years in the classroom.

Although assigning mentors to beginning teachers is not a particularly new approach to providing novice teachers with a support system, research points out that the impact of investments in induction and mentoring depends largely on whether they include very specific program characteristics (Smith & Ingersoll, 2004). For example, beginning teachers with access to a mentor in their subject area were approximately 30 percent less likely than teachers without a mentor to leave the profession after their first year. However, the logistics of ensuring one-to-one content-area matches as opposed to one content mentor serving multiple teachers often are more costly for school districts to implement and therefore tend not to be required in state policy.

Smith and Ingersoll's (2004) data also support providing new teachers with common planning time or scheduled collaboration with other teachers in their field. These induction activities reduce new teachers' risk of leaving the profession by approximately 43 percent.

Both characteristics of successful induction and mentoring programs can be heavily influenced by the principal. Identifying mentors who are a good match for new teachers, and seeking alternative solutions in case the match is not feasible within the existing composition of the faculty, are central to building a deep bench of instructional expertise at the school. Similarly, identifying creative uses of existing school-based time and resources for new and veteran teachers to engage in collaborative planning, observations, and professional learning communities is another critical local leadership skill that significantly influences the long-term success of state-level investments in beginning teacher support.

Of course, the characteristics of effective induction and mentoring programs also align with bigger financial investments on the part of states. As a result, states such as Illinois have phased in funding for robust induction programs through competitive grants to support pilot programs, with the hope of expanding funding to all districts in the future. Another approach employed by financially strapped states is to place the cost burden on the districts, which need to adhere to state-determined implementation guidelines if they want to continue to receive access to other sources of state funding for schools.

The number of states requiring some type of teacher induction program has increased markedly during the past several decades. Only eight states required induction in 1984, whereas today nearly all states require or support teacher induction in some way, with all of the thirty-six that applied for Race to the Top Phase II funding

> ### State Teacher Induction Initiatives
>
> Several states throughout the United States have designed and implemented statewide beginning teacher induction initiatives. Following are some of the highlights:
>
> - **Arizona.** In partnership with the Arizona K–12 Center, former governor Janet Napolitano developed and scaled up the Master Teacher Program, an initiative that grants full-time release to exemplary teachers to become mentors in high-need schools. All mentor-training sessions are funded, and each master teacher receives a $5,000 stipend.
> - **Oregon.** For the 2007–2009 biennial state budget, officials in Oregon appropriated $5 million for a statewide induction pilot.

proposing the strengthening of their teacher induction policies as a means to improve teacher effectiveness (Corcoran, 2007, p. 332; Goldrick, Osta, & Maddock, 2010, p. 3). Nearly half of the states fund statewide induction and mentoring programs for new teachers and require that certain standards for the selection, training, and matching of mentors and new teachers be met (Editorial Projects in Education, 2008). In Wisconsin, induction is required statewide during the five-year initial educator period, rather than being confined to a small-scale pilot program. The state has developed a Promising Programs induction model that districts are required to incorporate into their early educator support system. The model promotes ongoing orientation, support seminars, a qualified mentor for each initial educator who has been trained to provide input into his or her confidential formative assessment, and an administrator who has been trained in the state's Professional Development Plan team process. Alaska is unique in that its statewide mentoring program is full release, allowing master teachers to engage in full-time mentoring. As shown in the sidebar in this section, statewide induction programs also have been initiated recently in several states, including Arizona, Oregon, and Alabama. In other states, such as Minnesota, state policies encourage districts to provide induction and mentoring, but no requirements are in place. Induction programs for school principals and other administrators also have been developed in some states, including California, Maine, and Rhode Island.

A collaboration between the Oregon Department of Education, the Chalkboard Project, and the Boeing Company, Oregon's Educator Mentor Program offers support and resources to beginning teachers and administrators throughout the state. The program will be fully operational by the 2010–2011 school year.

- **Alabama.** In 2004, the Alabama State Board of Education resolved to adopt statewide standards for effective practice in the arena of induction and mentoring. Following this legislation, the Commission on Quality Teaching recommended that induction programs (which would include mentoring) be implemented in every district. Currently the Alabama Teacher Induction and Mentoring Program is fully authorized and funded.

- **Illinois.** Originally developed by the Illinois State Board of Education as a ten-district pilot, the Illinois New Teacher Collaborative brings induction to several locations throughout the state. Initially the state developed induction program guidelines, which served to align all induction programs with the state's guidance on quality mentoring and induction. In 2008 the state approved the Illinois Standards for Quality and Effectiveness for Beginning Teacher Induction Programs.

Engaging with the World Around You

The Use of Cultural Mentors in Hawaii

In 2005, the Hawaiian State Legislature voted to pass Act 159, which required the state's Department of Education to establish a state beginning teacher induction program. Though the act was meaningful in purpose, the state allocated no funding for the design and implementation of these new programs, and as a result induction in many places was never more than an idea. State Superintendent Patricia Hamamoto renewed the effort in early 2009, testifying before congress in favor of passing Senate Bill (SB) 738, which would establish and fund a Hawaii Beginning Teacher Induction Center (BTIC) pilot program that would "assist in the development and retention of highly qualified teachers in the state's public schools" (2009). The BTIC would, it was believed, aid drastically with Hawaii's teacher shortage and overall retention issues. Most recently, the Hawaii Department of Education has committed to establishing Induction Program Standards that will raise the quality of teacher induction in the state by

- Providing a three-year pathway of support to all new teachers in the state and a one-year pathway of support for experienced teachers who move to Hawaii to teach

- Securing a mentor for all beginning teachers in the state, ensuring that the mentor-to-teacher ratio does not exceed 1:15

- Equipping all beginning teachers with multiple opportunities to learn and grow through observations and coteaching experiences

- Requiring at least four formative evaluations and one summative evaluation for beginning teachers each year (Goldrick, Osta, & Maddock, 2010)

(This changed text updates the language about the old bill, which did not pass.) Simultaneous with this state-level action on academic mentoring, another initiative was beginning to gain momentum—one that focused on meeting the cultural needs of beginning teachers as well. In 2007, due to the results of a series of rounds of data collection on teacher needs, Walter Kahumoku was hired by the Kamehameha Schools—a network of private schools dedicated to serving the needs of native Hawaiian students—to work on professional development for the teachers of Hawaii. At the time, teacher attrition rates were high throughout the state, particularly in areas where the student body was largely made up of natives. Kahumoku believed that this attrition was greatly influenced by the cultural disconnect between the students and teachers in these areas; on average, native Hawaiians comprise 40 to 50 percent of the student body, but only 10 percent of the teaching force. With these numbers in mind, Kahumoku designed and implemented the Kahua Program, a mentoring program that serves as a complement to the academic induction already required by the state. By matching each beginning teacher with a cultural mentor, Kahua "provides a cultural lens to teaching and learning."

In practice, the Kahua Program pairs each new teacher with an elder from the community in which he or she teaches. The selection of these mentors is fairly simple, thanks to a preexisting program called Kupuna, in which community members visit elementary schools to teach native Hawaiian practices and mores. Before Kahua, Walter explains, the members of the Kupuna Education Center already were serving as informal "social and emotional mentors" to the new teachers. Now that Kahua has been operationalized, the mentees experience a two-day orientation to their (oftentimes brand-new) community, which is followed throughout the year with "seminar days" that are focused on curriculum and assessment, but with a cultural approach. When asked if the mentees stay in touch with their Kahua mentors, Kahumoku explains that they meet frequently, sometimes as often as twice a month. At the end of the year, each beginning teacher presents a Ho'ike, or final presentation, on all they have learned.

After the first year of Kahua's implementation, the attrition rate of new teachers at all Kamehameha schools dropped to only two. Because of this success, Kahumoku struck up a relationship with Complex Area Superintendent Mary Correa, who was interested in bringing the Kahua Program to life in some of Hawaii's public schools. At the time of this writing, Kahua serves seven of the fourteen complex areas throughout the state, on the islands of Hawaii, Maui, Molokai, and Oahu. Although not a by-product of the state policy on induction, the Kahua Program serves as a foundation of State Superintendent Patricia Hamamoto's recommendation that all teacher mentoring be guided by Hawaiian culture. And according to Walter Kahumoku, that is exactly the benefit of Kahua: "Now the acclimation to the area is a lot more smooth."

Clearly, induction is an area of great interest to states throughout the United States, an interest that generally is supported by research. Whether the support for implementing an induction and mentoring program originates at the state or local level, the research literature (Humphrey, Wechsler, & Bosetti, 2007; New Teacher Center, 2007; Smith & Ingersoll, 2004) supports the components of high-quality induction and mentoring programs described in the sidebar in this section. A high-quality induction program has a much better chance of being sustained over time, however, if it is connected to other investments in teacher retention such as strong school leadership. As this book has illustrated repeatedly, principals directly influence multiple aspects of teacher retention, including the ability to create a supportive workplace and ongoing assessment of teacher knowledge to identify the most appropriate professional development opportunities that will allow the novice teacher to continue to grow in confidence and skill.

HIGH-QUALITY PROFESSIONAL DEVELOPMENT: ENABLING TEACHERS

Access to federal Title I and Title II dollars actually provides states with a significant starting place to fund professional development, and in some states those are the only dollars earmarked to support continuing teacher education. However, one of the downsides of the less restricted use of Title II dollars in particular is that many school districts have opted to apply those resources to reducing class size, as opposed to investing in high-quality professional learning for existing teachers. In addition to overseeing the distribution of federal monies that can be allocated to districts and schools for teacher professional development, states have other important leadership responsibilities for ensuring access to professional development, as follows:

- States can develop policies that set the parameters for funding, implementation, and quality, in addition to requirements related to recertification, which can have a significant effect on the types of professional development offered.

- State education agency (SEA) staff with oversight for specific content or curricular areas often provide guidance to school and districts on developing in-service days; evening, weekend, or summer programs; and teacher course credit options.

- SEAs manage other school improvement and reform priorities that further impact funding for school and district professional development options, such as the development of state standards for teaching and learning, the review of textbooks and curriculum materials, and school improvement strategies for low-performing schools and districts (adapted from Blank, de las Alas, & Smith, 2008, p. 4).

- **Mentor selection.** The selection of mentors must be rigorous and based on explicit qualities—such as strong communication skills and trustworthiness—and teachers and mentors should teach in the same field.

- **Support for mentors.** If mentors are to effectively support new teachers, they need certain supports, including ongoing professional development on effective mentoring.

- **Interactions between mentors and new teachers.** Sanctioned time should be set aside for mentors and new teachers to interact on a regular basis (either weekly or biweekly); this interaction should be connected to the development of a schoolwide learning community.

- **Basis of learning.** The guidance provided to new teachers should be based on data and professional teaching standards.

- **Involvement of administrators.** The involvement and support of school administrators is crucial, and their roles and responsibilities should be clearly defined.

- **Involvement of other stakeholders.** All stakeholders should be involved in the development of a new teacher induction and mentoring program.

Nevertheless, unlike many other economically advanced societies, the United States generally does not provide the sustained, in-depth, subject-specific professional development that is common in other countries (Wei, Darling-Hammond, Andree, Richardson, & Orphanos, 2009). The typical continuing professional development program for teachers in the United States includes one-shot, large-group presentations that last only a few hours, despite research that identifies program length as one key predictor of teacher learning in professional settings (Cohen & Hill, 2001). Similarly, reimbursement for teachers who engage in graduate coursework is another common use for local professional development dollars, despite growing evidence that this type of investment in a teacher's continuing education is not aligned to school improvement goals and has not been found to improve instructional practice or student achievement (Clotfelter, Ladd, & Vigdor, 2006). Unfortunately, sound principles of professional development such as those listed in the sidebar in this section rarely are applied in continuing professional development for teachers (Corcoran, 1995; Heibert, 1999). Lack of research-based evidence in support of many professional development offerings affects both the supply of and demand for ongoing education for teachers. In addition, the ability to make research-based decisions about high-quality investments in professional development with and for teachers is typically not emphasized in administrator preparation programs.

For example, Birman, Desimone, Porter, and Garet (2000) surveyed a nationally representative sample of teachers who participated in professional development funded by Title II of ESEA as amended by the No Child Left Behind Act. Their report identified three structural features (form, duration, and participation) and three core features (content focus, active learning, and coherence) that establish the context for high-quality professional development. Their results indicate that the number of teachers who participate in professional development that addresses all six characteristics is moderately low. Of the respondents, 79 percent indicated they had participated in the "traditional" form of professional development, and most teachers (64 percent) had participated in activities that lasted only a week or less. In terms of collective participation, relatively few teachers (20 percent) had participated in professional development with colleagues within their school or department.

Although the state can provide funding and general guidelines on access, delivery, and implementation of professional development, it frequently is principals and teachers who make the final decisions about where and how to invest these scarce resources. The research on what constitutes effective professional development is significant, but the actual number of providers who can claim measurable effects of their specific programs on student outcomes, teacher knowledge, or teacher instructional practices is small by comparison. Of the 25 professional development programs for teachers of mathematics and science used in 14 different states, only 7 programs were found to have measurable effects on students, 10 of the studies demonstrated effects on teacher knowledge, and 4 studies had a demonstrable impact on instructional practices of teachers (Blank et al., 2008). As a result, it is no wonder that the primary consumers of professional development—teachers and principals—invest in unproven strategies for improving teaching and learning. Nevertheless, a school leader, at a minimum, can commit to ensuring that decisions about professional development resource allocation meet the following criteria: they are closely tied to school improvement goals, they include multiple opportunities for participants to engage with the material, and in most cases they are tied to developing content-based expertise. Similarly, SEAs can provide guidance to school leaders through the development of statewide standards for professional development, online databases of approved providers who have evidence of their program's impact on teacher knowledge, practice, and, ideally, student learning.

A Systematic Approach to Professional Development in Maryland

In May 2002, Dr. Colleen Seremet was hired to be Maryland's assistant state superintendent for instruction. She was brought on board by State Superintendent Dr. Nancy Grasmick to implement both a new assessment system and a new voluntary state curriculum. As she began to plan for the rollout of these new programs, she knew that gaining the buy-in of teachers would be crucial to success. Seremet said to Grasmick: "This is all well and good, but if teachers can't use this curriculum to help their kids on this assessment, we've got a problem. There's a third side to this triangle, and it's the teacher professional development side." And just like that, Seremet began to focus her work on professional development (PD).

At the time, teachers viewed PD in Maryland as "largely a waste of time." Seremet explained that on the whole it did not include the elements necessary for a high-quality system: it was not differentiated or on target. Because of these feelings, State Superintendent Grasmick initiated the Maryland Professional Development Advisory Council (PDAC) in January 2003. The group originally was composed of representatives from many stakeholder groups: members of the higher education community, the Maryland State Department of Education, each of the state's twenty-four school districts, principals, union leaders, teachers, county commissioners, and the parent teacher association. Once she had everyone at the table, Grasmick charged the group with two tasks:

1. Report on the state of teacher professional development in Maryland
2. Define "high-quality professional development"

To accomplish the first of the two charges, the PDAC developed a project called Mapping the State and Local Infrastructure for Teacher Professional Development. To collect data for this study, the group conducted interviews at both the district and state levels and disseminated a survey to capture the current design and implementation of PD in Maryland. The survey included examples of different types of professional development opportunities (such as university coursework, district workshops, school-based coaching, peer study groups, and action research) and asked teachers to rate their experiences against a series of quality-control indicators. In order for an experience to be categorized as "high quality," it had to meet fifteen of the seventeen possible indicators. Of the state's total 56,000 teachers, 39,000 completed the online survey, and the results, which can be found in the PDAC's first report, showed that only 35 percent of teachers were participating in at least one activity that met the high-quality benchmark. Although this low number was disappointing at first,

Seremet reported that it was a true impetus for change. "As for implications," she said, "interestingly, using a rigorous definition of quality and going straight to the teachers was just what we needed to get things going."

As for the second task, Seremet explained, the council developed a definition of professional development that is both broad and specific. It includes and accounts for multiple non-school-based activities. Seremet explained that there were serious implications in this work on assigning "high quality" to out-of-school supports but that the council was very thoughtful about this process and did nothing without full consensus. From there, "The council took it as an opportunity to write its own standards." As preparation for this process, the council reviewed twenty-six sets of standards, including the National Staff Development Council's professional development standards, which were guiding Maryland's PD at the time. Once the new Maryland standards had been drafted, the PDAC took to the streets, holding seventy focus groups throughout the state to receive public comment. These focus groups were largely positive, as those stakeholders interviewed did not suggest any major changes to the standards themselves. Instead, questions began to arise regarding motivation and implementation. In Seremet's words, "The big message from the focus groups was, 'So, do you really believe this? Are people really going to change?'" These hard-hitting and honest questions prompted a set of recommendations, which initiated the development of a suite of tools. District and school officials now can go to the Maryland PDAC web site to find both a six-step planning guide and an evaluation guide. The first piece guides policymakers through the process of designing and implementing high-quality professional development for teachers. The second, even though it does not mandate *how* to evaluate PD programs, helps districts better assess *when* to evaluate. In Seremet's words, "We approach this not from a regulatory perspective, but from a collegial 'We all have to learn how to do this work better' perspective."

When asked about the future of PD for teachers in the state of Maryland, Seremet simultaneously celebrates the work done thus far and acknowledges that there is much left to do. "If you're serious about PD," she quipped, "you have to honestly say to yourself that most of the people doing the work need a lot of scaffolding. It's not about the inputs or the quality of the learning activities; it's about what the teachers learned and how you know they learned it." And with this attitude running statewide, she is confident that Maryland is headed in the right direction.

MAKING CONNECTIONS TO INDUCTION, MENTORING, AND PROFESSIONAL DEVELOPMENT ACROSS THE CAREER CONTINUUM

As the discussion of the research and policy base supporting high-quality induction, mentoring, and professional development in this chapter demonstrates, states play an increasingly important role in ensuring connections across key policy components along the educator's career continuum. State budget cycles often force policymakers to make incremental decisions that might result in reduced funding for one program, such as professional development, while increasing support for a statewide induction model. For this reason, it is critically important that clear goals for improving educator effectiveness are articulated and communicated broadly, so that education stakeholder groups—and especially school-level leaders—continuously can remind state policymakers of the need to align investments to state goals for improvement and to connect programs and practice across the educator's career continuum.

The rubric that follows can assist state policymakers in thinking systemically about new policy support and investments in educator effectiveness. But given that state policymakers are not always in a position to address multiple components along the educator's career continuum in a coordinated manner, school and district leaders can make adjustments locally to ensure the necessary connections that lead to more efficient and effective use of resources, which in turn will result in a more robust learning environment for the adults, and especially for the students. For example, district leaders can ensure that preparation programs seamlessly transition into an induction and mentoring program. And principals can ensure that professional development opportunities are connected to assessments of teacher performance and that teachers have access to high-quality mentors and opportunities to improve their practice.

Rubric 4.1. Is Your Plan for Securing Effective Teachers Through Induction and Ongoing Professional Development Connected to and Complemented by the Other Key Educator Talent Management Areas?

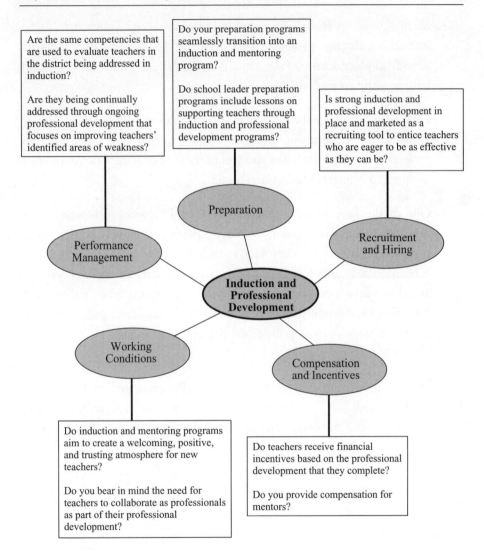

Are the same competencies that are used to evaluate teachers in the district being addressed in induction?

Are they being continually addressed through ongoing professional development that focuses on improving teachers' identified areas of weakness?

Do your preparation programs seamlessly transition into an induction and mentoring program?

Do school leader preparation programs include lessons on supporting teachers through induction and professional development programs?

Is strong induction and professional development in place and marketed as a recruiting tool to entice teachers who are eager to be as effective as they can be?

Preparation

Performance Management

Recruitment and Hiring

Induction and Professional Development

Working Conditions

Compensation and Incentives

Do induction and mentoring programs aim to create a welcoming, positive, and trusting atmosphere for new teachers?

Do you bear in mind the need for teachers to collaborate as professionals as part of their professional development?

Do teachers receive financial incentives based on the professional development that they complete?

Do you provide compensation for mentors?

From the Statehouse to the Schoolhouse: Getting the Ball Rolling

1. Many schools in Hawaii have decided to incorporate Kahua mentoring into their induction programs as a supplement to the academic mentors already in place. Can you see benefits that a program such as this would have in your area as well?

2. How prescriptive are the induction and mentoring policies in your state? What is the relationship between those policies and the induction program at your school? Do you feel that the state is supportive of your design and implementation decisions?

3. One of the key elements of the Maryland Professional Development Advisory Council is its comprehensive participant list. In soliciting input from many different stakeholder groups, the Maryland Department of Education was able to simultaneously tap into many useful resources and drum up support for their induction and professional development initiative. How might you work to build these relationships in your own state? Do your current policies on professional development allow for feedback-inspired revisions?

4. How is professional development currently evaluated in your state? At the school level? And district level? Does your state policy include language about the design and implementation of an evaluation system?

RESEARCH-BASED POLICIES THAT SUPPORT MENTORING, INDUCTION, AND PROFESSIONAL DEVELOPMENT: HOW IS YOUR STATE DOING?

A. Induction and Mentorship	Yes	No	N/A
1. Does your state require high-quality mentoring for all new teachers?	☐	☐	☐
Does it ensure that criteria for effective mentors (such as mentor training and mentor selection) are met?	☐	☐	☐
Does it ensure that mentoring is of sufficient length and frequency to meet the needs of new teachers?	☐	☐	☐
2. Does your state require a complete and individualized induction program for new teachers?	☐	☐	☐
3. Does your state support districts in ensuring appropriate, manageable teaching assignments for new teachers?	☐	☐	☐
Does it require that new teachers be assigned classes within their area of licensure?	☐	☐	☐
Does it give new teachers novice status?	☐	☐	☐
Does it require that new teachers be given a manageable number of classes for which to prepare?	☐	☐	☐
Does it require that new teachers be assigned classes of reasonable sizes?	☐	☐	☐
B. Professional Development	**Yes**	**No**	**N/A**
1. Does your state support ongoing, job-embedded, and differentiated professional development for all teachers?	☐	☐	☐
2. Does your state align professional development with the state's school improvement goals or vision?	☐	☐	☐
3. Does your state monitor the effectiveness of the professional development provided?	☐	☐	☐

REFERENCES

Alabama Teacher Induction and Mentoring Program. Retrieved April 29, 2010, from http://www.alsde.edu/Search/Default.aspx.

Arizona Master Teacher Program. Retrieved April 29, 2010, from http://www.azk12.org/content/mt.

Birman, B. F., Desimone, L., Porter, A. C., & Garet, M. S. (2000). Designing professional development that works. *Educational Leadership, 57*(8), 28–33.

Blank, R., de las Alas, N., & Smith, C. (2008). *Does professional development have effects on teaching and learning?* Washington, DC: Council of Chief State School Officers.

Clotfelter, C., Ladd, H. F., & Vigdor, J. L. (2006). *Teacher-student matching and the assessment of teacher effectiveness* (NBER Working Paper No. 11936). Cambridge, MA: National Bureau of Academic Research.

Cohen, D., & Hill, H. (2001). *Learning policy: When state education reform works.* New Haven, CT: Yale University Press.

Corcoran, T. C. (1995). *Transforming professional development for teachers: A guide for state policymakers.* Washington, DC: National Governors Association. Retrieved September 3, 2009, from http://www.aecf.org/upload/PublicationFiles/ED3622H115.pdf.

Corcoran, T. B. (2007). The changing and chaotic world of teacher policy. In S. H. Fuhrman, D. K. Cohen, & F. Mosher (Eds.), *The state of education policy research* (pp. 307–336). Philadelphia: Erlbaum.

Editorial Projects in Education. (2008). Quality counts 2008: Tapping into teaching [Special issue]. *Education Week, 27*(18).

Glazerman, S., Isenberg, E., Dolfin, S., Bleeker, M., Johnson, A., Grider, M., & Jacobus, M. (2010). *Impacts of comprehensive teacher induction: Final Results from a randomized controlled study—executive summary* (NCEE 2010–4028). Washington, DC: National Center for Education Evaluation and Regional Assistance. Retrieved August 27, 2010, from http://ies.ed.gov/ncee/pubs/20104027/pdf/20104028.pdf.

Goldrick, L., Osta, D., & Maddock, A. (2010). Race to the Top: Phase two. Teacher induction and teaching and learning conditions. Santa Cruz, CA: New Teacher Center. Retrieved August 27, 2010, from http://www.newteachercenter.org/pdfs/RaceToTheTop_Phase2_NewTeacherCenter.pdf.

Grissmer, D., & Kirby, S. (1997). Teacher turnover and teacher quality. *Teachers College Record, 99*, 45–46.

Heibert, J. (1999). Relationships between research and the NCTM standards. *Journal for Research in Mathematics Education, 30*(1), 3–19.

Humphrey, D. C., Wechsler, M. E., & Bosetti, K. R. (2007). *Teacher induction in Illinois and Ohio: A preliminary analysis.* Menlo Park, CA: SRI International. Retrieved September 3, 2009, from http://policyweb.sri.com/cep/publications/TeacherInductioninIllinoisandOhio-Feb2007.pdf.

Illinois New Teacher Collaborative. Retrieved April 29, 2010, from http://intc .education.illinois.edu.

National Commission on Excellence in Education (1983). *A nation at risk: The imperative for educational reform.* Washington, DC: Government Printing Office.

National Commission on Teaching and America's Future. (1997). *Doing what matters most: Investing in quality teaching.* New York: National Commission on Teaching and America's Future.

New Teacher Center (2007). *High-quality mentoring and induction practices.* Santa Cruz, CA: Author. Retrieved September 3, 2009, from http://www .newteachercenter.org/pdfs/Cap_Hill_HQM_final.pdf.

Oregon Educator Mentor Program. Retrieved April 29, 2010, from http:// www.mentoringeducators.org/about-us.php.

Smith, T. M., & Ingersoll, R. M. (2004). What are the effects of induction and mentoring on beginning teacher turnover? *American Educational Research Journal, 41*(3), 681–714.

Wei, R. C., Darling-Hammond, L., Andree, A., Richardson, N., & Orphanos, S. (2009). *Professional learning in the learning profession: A status report on teacher development in the United States and abroad* (Technical Report). Dallas, TX: National Staff Development Council. Retrieved March 17, 2010, from http://www.nsdc.org/news/ NSDCstudytechnicalreport2009.pdf.

CHAPTER FIVE

Setting the Table

The Role of Institutions of Higher Education in Preparing Teachers for Success

The incoming class of teacher candidates have started their preparation course, and you have to say you are impressed—they are an intelligent, motivated, friendly, and dedicated group. "Why are these alarmists carrying on about teacher quality?" you ask yourself as you sip your coffee and pick up the newspaper. But then you see the headline: "50 Percent of Teachers Quitting Within Five Years." You head to your office, determined to take action so that that your preparation program does not contribute to this problem, but rather becomes a model solution for the role of higher education in creating a world-class teaching force. But, you wonder, what exactly does this solution entail?

OVERVIEW

The previous chapters of this book have looked at how teacher recruitment, induction, development, working conditions, compensation, and evaluation can be improved through strategic, comprehensive action by school and district leaders, state policymakers, and teachers' unions. This chapter explores the role of institutions of higher education (IHEs) in systemic educator talent management.

Teacher preparation often is seen as a separate entity from schools' and districts' efforts to recruit, retain, and develop teachers. Yet leaders at schools and districts who seek to promote systemic teacher-quality policymaking need to recognize that what happens in teacher preparation is not necessarily outside their realm of influence and is certainly relevant to their efforts to improve teacher quality. As instructional leaders, school principals and other administrators must understand what takes place in IHEs and work to fill gaps in teachers' knowledge through their own interactions with teachers and, over the long term, by influencing what takes place during preservice training. Similarly, as key players in teacher hiring decisions, school leaders need to know and influence the quality of candidates emerging from different IHE programs.

There are approximately 1,300 IHE and alternative-route programs that prepare roughly 185,000 new teachers each year in the United States (Reschly, Holdheide, Behrstock, & Weber, 2009). In preparing teachers, IHEs greatly influence the quality of the teaching profession in these two key ways:

1. IHEs serve as a gateway to the profession. They determine who to accept into their programs and who may graduate. In many cases, IHEs have partnerships with school districts, influencing to some degree where their graduates find employment.

2. IHEs prepare candidates to be effective in the classroom. IHEs set the tone for the rest of a teacher's career and equip them to be successful in the classroom. By effectively teaching candidates the range of pedagogical and content knowledge and skills through coursework and field experiences, IHEs enable their graduates to effectively teach children from day one in the classroom.

Eighty percent of new teachers feel that as a result of their preparation programs they were very (42 percent) or somewhat (38 percent) prepared for the classroom (National Comprehensive Center for Teacher Quality & Public Agenda, 2008). But IHEs have also been criticized as often being too theoretical, insufficient to meet the needs of diverse learners, and otherwise inadequate (Levine, 2006). In addition, there is some evidence that teachers are underprepared for some of the challenges of teaching that most detrimentally affect teacher attrition. For example, a recent study in Chicago found that the schools with the highest rates of teacher turnover were those with the greatest problems with school safety and parental engagement (Allensworth, Ponisciak, & Mazzeo, 2009). Yet only 78 percent of new teachers' preparation programs covered classroom management and maintaining discipline, and only 51 percent covered working with parents and community members. Moreover, although the vast majority of teachers whose preparation programs covered these issues found it at least a little helpful, only 58 percent believed their preparation in classroom management helped them "a lot," and 41 percent believed their preparation in community and parental engagement helped them "a lot" once in the classroom (National Comprehensive Center for Teacher Quality & Public Agenda, 2008).

This information clearly suggests that IHE and alternative-route programs have some changes to make in the training of their teachers. But it also has implications for school principals and other leaders who wish to provide leadership and build teachers' knowledge in skills in these critical but underdeveloped areas. In addition, there are implications for the types of ongoing professional development activities that should be promoted by districts.

This chapter will highlight strategies that you can use related to IHEs and how to include IHEs in a systemic approach to improving teacher quality. The chapter will focus on preservice teacher preparation, but it should be noted that teacher preparation increasingly is seen as an activity that, as in professions like medicine or law, is ongoing throughout a teacher's career.

SERVE AS A GATEWAY TO THE PROFESSION

Although it is not their primary function, IHEs critically affect teacher quality by serving as the gateway into the profession. In this capacity, they determine who to accept into their programs and who may graduate. The selectivity of teacher preparation programs can greatly affect the quality of the profession (National Council for Accreditation of Teacher Education, 2008; Singh & Stoloff, 2008; Walsh & Jacobs, 2007).

In the McKinsey & Company report *How the World's Best-Performing School Systems Come Out on Top*, it was found that a key issue that differentiated the world's strongest education systems from weaker ones was the selectivity of teacher preparation programs. The report stated: "The top-performing school systems consistently attract more able people into the teaching profession, leading to better student outcomes. They do this by making entry to teacher training highly selective, developing effective processes for selecting the right applicants to become teachers. . . . The top-performing systems select for entry into the teacher training programs. They do so either by controlling entry directly, or by limiting the number of places on teacher training courses, so that supply matches demand. . . . Making teacher training selective in this manner makes it attractive to high performers" (Barber & Mourshed, 2007).

In many of the top-performing systems in other countries, a smaller number of teacher training places are available, but these are funded by the public education system so that top-performing candidates are incentivized to follow through with their decisions to become teachers. By contrast, in the United States, teacher preparation programs often are seen as the "cash cow" of IHEs because they admit large numbers of applicants and charge them a tuition that may be disproportionately high compared to the cost of delivering the course. This large student intake often is accompanied by lenient admissions standards.

Although this approach may generate revenue for IHEs, it does not improve the quality of teaching that students will encounter in their classrooms. The lack of selectivity not only lowers the prestige of the profession and the level of learning that may take place in courses, but also is unfair to program participants, who may invest large sums of money in tuition for a program that may not lead to employment in their field. If IHEs accept candidates who are not likely to complete the program successfully, or if they graduate more candidates than there are positions for, these training teachers may find themselves out of money and without added employability. At some teacher preparation programs, as few as 60 percent of graduates actually find full-time employment within a year of graduation, with other graduates resorting to substitute positions or jobs in other fields (Snelgrove, 2009).

It is the responsibility of all involved in teacher policymaking to help avert teacher unemployment in those fields where surpluses typically emerge (for example, English/language arts, social studies, physical education, art, and elementary education). In many states, an annual or biannual teacher supply-and-demand report is produced, which highlights the subject areas that exhibit shortages or surpluses. By encouraging IHE officials to use these to read the labor market and make admissions decisions accordingly, you can contribute to a greater match between teacher supply and demand. In England, for example, a complex national teacher supply-and-demand model is used annually to estimate the number of new teachers that will be needed to fully staff all positions in each subject area. Because the government funds the large majority of teacher training tuition, it requires higher education institutions to limit their admissions for each subject to the number that the model specifies. Although such central planning may not be possible or even appropriate in the United States, IHEs should at least *try* to read the market to the extent possible, so that teachers who are admitted to their programs are likely to be able to find employment in their field.

Moreover, the various stakeholders in the system can be further brought together if school leaders, districts, and IHEs work jointly to read the local or regional market, sharing insights on fields where applications and applicant quality are high and areas where they are not. School districts and IHEs should form relationships to jointly analyze the market, bringing school leaders who are involved in the hiring process into the discussions as well. In addition to providing information about areas of teacher shortage and surplus, such partnerships between districts, school leaders, and IHEs can facilitate the recruitment and hiring process for teachers who wish to remain in the area.

Although IHEs serve as the gateway to the profession, their responsibilities do not end there. Rather, IHEs should be partners in teacher induction and mentoring and ongoing professional development. In this way, the role of IHEs spans the teacher career continuum and forms an integral part of any comprehensive and systemic approach to improving teacher quality. School leaders should facilitate this role and act as partners in delivering this ongoing support.

Teacher Residencies

Strategic Recruitment and Preparation of Teachers

Teacher residencies present a novel approach to preparing teachers, and Urban Teacher Residency United (UTRU) is paving the way for this model to be brought to scale. In addition to improving teacher recruitment, retention, and the quality of teacher preparation, residency programs demonstrate how districts, schools, and IHEs can work together—and not at cross-purposes—to strategically recruit the types of teachers that are in greatest demand.

When Anissa Listak, managing director of UTRU, and others launched the initiative in 2007, the goal was to expand and enhance the quality of new residency programs in light of the much-documented success of pioneer programs including Chicago's Academy for Urban School Leadership, the Boston Teacher Residency, and Denver's Boettcher Teachers Program.

Residency programs involve a rigorous candidate selection process, master-degree-level course work, an intensive year-long classroom apprenticeship to a trained mentor, and access to a coach in subsequent years when the residents take on their own classrooms. Typically, a school district, university, and/or nonprofit organization will partner to develop a residency. The cross-organizational design team will attend UTRU's Residency for Residencies Program to learn all there is to know for emerging programs to be successful in preparing teachers.

The residency model is unique in that school districts and/or nonprofit organizations serve as the lever to form partnerships with IHEs, typically by issuing a request for proposal for IHEs that are willing and able to work with them in this capacity. Listak said: "The ability to recruit teachers in partnership is the value-added for the district. . . . Districts love that they can really home-grow the teachers that are needed." The residency model goes beyond only finding great teachers for the district—this model finds great teachers in the areas where they are most needed.

In Boston, for example, the district and the Boston Teacher Residency convene twelve months prior to teacher hiring phases to discuss which types of teachers—in terms of subject area, grade level, and demographic factors (such as gender or ethnic background)—are needed, and the Boston Teacher Residency recruits teachers accordingly. This aids schools and districts while simultaneously averting cases of teacher unemployment. "We encourage our partner programs to be in service to the district by training only the teachers the district needs," said Listak.

Because of their reputation as high-quality preparation experiences and their marketing efforts, residency programs often are better able than local school districts to recruit the specific types of candidates needed.

In addition, teacher residency programs work to create resident learning standards that drive program implementation. These standards focus on the knowledge, skills, and dispositions that residents need in order to become highly effective urban educators. Throughout the residency year, there are both practical experiences through the classroom apprenticeship to a mentor teacher and theoretical experiences through the master-degree-level course work that help to reinforce the resident learning standards. These experiences ensure that teacher candidates are indeed learning the skills and knowledge that are believed to be most relevant for entering the teaching profession.

Although the focus of UTRU is on urban classrooms, the model set for district, school leader, and IHE conversations and actions related to strategic teacher recruitment is one that applies to rural, suburban, and urban school settings alike.

Source: A. Listak, managing director, Urban Teacher Residency United, personal communication, February 25, 2010.

PREPARE CANDIDATES TO BE EFFECTIVE IN THE CLASSROOM

Whether your IHE provides a five-week intensive, alternative-route preparation program or a four-year undergraduate preparation program, you know that not even an hour of time devoted to learning to be an effective teacher should be wasted on irrelevant activities when there is so much crucial material to cover. Teachers must engage in course work and clinical experiences that equip them to use effective pedagogy to engage and teach content to students with diverse learning needs and from diverse cultural backgrounds.

First and foremost, you can help ensure that your IHE is meeting its responsibility to equip teachers with the skills and knowledge they need to effectively teach their students the necessary content. These skills should be taught through both course work and clinical experiences, which should be aligned with one another and with the program mission and state standards (Bouck,

2005). Preparation programs should combine academic grounding with practice-based training and continued learning to equip new teachers with the knowledge and skills they need to begin the complex practice of teaching (Alter & Coggshall, 2009).

Certainly, no individual teacher can learn *everything*, and there is a real need for schools, districts, and states to transform traditional staffing models to meet the needs of twenty-first-century schools. This involves teachers, like other professionals, no longer being viewed as generalists, but rather as specialists who work together as colleagues to see that all the learning needs of all students are met via instruction by a true expert in the area (Coggshall & Lasagna, 2009). While promoting such a transformation of staffing, IHEs should at the very least introduce all teachers to the key instructional practices that they or their colleagues need to employ to be effective. Specifically, both preparation coursework and clinical experiences should enhance teachers' skills and knowledge along the following lines:

The need for general and special education teachers to implement evidence-based instructional practices, especially in teaching early reading, is emphasized in the reauthorization of the Elementary and Secondary Education Act (the No Child Left Behind Act of 2001). Teachers are more likely to be successful in raising student achievement if they use specific teaching interventions that research has identified as effective (Kavale, 2005).

IHEs must help teachers to master specific techniques for teaching content to students with a variety of special learning needs to close achievement gaps and effectively teach today's increasingly diverse school population. The proportion of English language learners in schools is now 10 percent (National Clearinghouse for English Language Acquisition, 2010). Meanwhile, the integration of special needs students into general classrooms has become more commonplace (Whitten & Rodriguez-Campos, 2003). Being able to effectively teach English language learners, children from culturally diverse backgrounds, children from deprived backgrounds, gifted children, and children with any number of learning disabilities is a must for many of today's teachers. Classes should provide training in multicultural awareness (Bouck, 2005). Opportunities for general education and special education teacher candidates to collaborate should be provided (Blanton & Pugach,

2007). Furthermore, clinical education experiences should include high-needs schools and classrooms (Barley, 2009).

In addition, *prospective teachers need to learn how to identify and immediately address problems with individual students' achievement* because even the best teacher instruction is unlikely to cover all gaps. Response to intervention (RTI) is becoming increasingly recognized as an effective method for addressing academic failure and is encouraged within the Individuals with Disabilities Education Act. RTI involves frequent student assessment, early intervention where problems are identified, and progressively more intense interventions as and when needed (Reschly & Bergstrom, 2009). By teaching teachers to respond to student learning needs in this way, IHEs move toward improving teacher quality.

Likewise, *prospective teachers need to learn how to identify and use research* so that they can continually improve their instructional practice as and when research advances the understanding of what works in the classroom. IHEs are often the closest source of access to research and researchers that teachers will receive during their careers, and it is therefore important that IHEs take advantage of their proximity during the teacher preparation phase as well as build pathways for teachers to continually access the latest relevant research throughout their careers.

A recent study of teachers' use of educational research found that although teachers hold mixed positive and negative views of research, they are by no means categorically disinclined to using educational research to improve their practice and are particularly inclined to seek out research when they have an immediate pressing concern. Yet a number of barriers—from time and cost to skepticism that the findings apply to their contexts—prevent teachers from using research as much as they would like (Behrstock, Drill, & Miller, 2009). The researchers conclude that teacher preparation programs play an important role in building the foundations for a research-oriented teaching career by shaping teachers' views and approaches to using research to improve their instruction. They recommend that IHEs do the following:

- Bridge the gap between teachers and researchers so that the two groups build trust and share knowledge. This can be accomplished, for example, through joint seminars, coffee hours, or project work.

- Teach teachers how to locate research on effective instructional practices. This includes training in using search engines effectively, interpreting the findings, and determining the credibility of the research they review.

- Maintain contact with teachers after they enter the classroom in order to assist and encourage them in accessing evidence-based information that is relevant to their needs (Behrstock, Drill, & Miller, 2009).

Equally important to these changes at the IHE level is that school and district leaders facilitate teachers' research use. The report suggests that teachers would be far more likely to read research that was filtered by their department chair, school administrators, or the district because they trust that the research vetted in this manner would be of high quality and relevant to their particular teaching context (for example, the specific needs of limited English proficiency learners and diverse learners). In addition to filtering research for teachers' use, school and district leaders can promote opportunities for teachers to collaborate on research use, such as structured study groups.

Finally, *IHEs should prepare teachers to deal with some of the nonacademic challenges that teachers claim are highly important,* along with effective pedagogy as a means to improve teacher quality. For example, as mentioned above, a study by the Consortium on Chicago School Research found that parental engagement with *teachers* (as opposed to only parental engagement with their children, for example) was important (Allensworth et al., 2009). This finding was corroborated in a recent survey by Public Agenda and Learning Point Associates (2009), which found that parental involvement was viewed by teachers as among the most important factors that could improve the teaching profession. Among Gen Y teachers (those born between 1977 and 1995), parental involvement was cited by more than twice as many teachers as any other factor likely to improve the teaching profession. You should therefore encourage your teacher preparation program leaders to include strategies for working effectively with parents.

Likewise, study after study confirms that teachers unanimously agree that student discipline and motivation influence their effectiveness and their morale (see, among others, DeAngelis, Peddle, Trott, & Bergeron, 2002; Ingersoll & Smith, 2003; and the National Comprehensive Center for Teacher Quality & Public Agenda, 2007). Still, it is not uncommon for parents and students to attribute misbehavior and lack of interest to the effectiveness of the *teacher* in engaging them sufficiently. IHEs should incorporate strategies both on engaging unmotivated students and on effectively addressing disciplinary problems and managing the classroom.

In teaching teachers these strategies, you ought to encourage those at your IHE to employ a variety of teaching methods, such as case studies, video and hypermedia, logs, journals, diaries, reflective reports, practitioner research, and autobiographical sketches (Darling-Hammond & Baratz-Snowden, 2005).

Having decided what and how to teach teachers what they need to know to be effective in the classroom, IHEs must continually monitor how well they are in fact achieving this and then take steps toward continually improving their programs (Blanton & Pugach, 2007). IHEs may ask the following questions:

- Are IHEs obtaining constructive feedback from candidates about the quality of their teacher preparation programs? Are IHEs obtaining feedback after graduation *and* again after teachers have spent considerable time in the classroom?
- Are IHEs obtaining information about the effectiveness of their graduates in the classroom?
- Are IHEs using the data received from teachers and other sources to make continual improvements to the quality of their preparation programs?
- Are IHEs involving all major stakeholder groups in the evaluation and improvement of their programs?
- What barriers prevent IHEs from making further improvements, and how might IHEs overcome these challenges?

Certain tools and activities can aid this process of self-evaluation. One example is the use of innovation configurations, which assist IHE faculty in assessing the extent to which evidence-based practices currently are prevalent in their coursework and supervision. Innovation configurations then encourage collaboration in targeting program improvement, as well as IHE faculty training (Reschly et al., 2009).

Another example is the engagement of consortia of IHEs in statewide or regionwide evaluations of the performance of graduates from each institution once on the job. In Illinois, the Association of Deans of Public Colleges of Education launched the Illinois Teacher Graduate Assessment project in 2004 to collect data on how prepared and how satisfied first-year teachers emerging from various preparation programs are. Collected annually, these data serve the following purposes:

- Assess teacher graduates' views in a standardized way across the state
- Assess teachers' skills as they relate to the Illinois Professional Teaching Standards and the Illinois Learning Standards
- Provide IHEs with information on the effectiveness of their programs for preparing teachers to facilitate efforts to improve their courses
- Provide the public and policymakers with information about teacher preparation for accountability purposes

In Illinois, these surveys indicated that IHEs ought to consider enhancing their preparation programs in the areas of English language learners, administrators, parents, and the community (Lucas, 2009).

Meanwhile, school leaders, for their part, should work simultaneously to fill gaps in their teachers' skills and knowledge that were not addressed in the preparation stage and communicate with IHEs and alternative-route programs about their perceptions of needed program reforms.

Assessing Teacher Preparation by Assessing Teacher Performance

At the University of Washington and Stanford University, teacher preparation is inextricably linked with the broader teacher career continuum through a performance assessment system that is being developed collaboratively with a consortium of states and school and district leaders. The Teacher Performance Assessment Consortium has created multiple assessments to aid schools, districts, states, and IHEs with teacher licensure, tenure, ongoing evaluation, and career development.

It is well known by all education stakeholders that at various junctures in a teacher's career it is necessary to assess his or her performance, but that rigorous, high-quality assessment instruments for doing so are lacking. After all, assessing the complex art of teaching is complicated, with outcomes-based and input-driven measures, disagreement on the definition of effectiveness in teaching, and with any individual teacher's use of effective practices varying from day to day and lesson to lesson. But the Teacher Performance Assessment Consortium faced these challenges head-on, convening a national design team to develop assessments whose psychometric quality exceeds that of existing instruments.

The assessments benefit everybody because they are geared toward both supporting teachers and judging their teaching performance. As Professor Ken Zeichner, director of teacher education at the University of Washington, stated: "We are making the assessment a valuable professional development experience, rather than a hoop to jump through. . . . We provide support for teacher candidates to get through this assessment. It's a curriculum issue, and it's a professional development and learning issue."

These assessments are useful not only for evaluating teachers' readiness to enter the profession and their performance at various stages across the career continuum, but also for evaluating the quality of teacher preparation programs by analyzing the preparedness of their graduates. At the University of Washington, this works in the following manner. First, an individual is employed to compile the performance assessment data collected and coordinate the analysis, and then the faculty members sit down with a K–12 advisory group composed of cooperating teachers, principals, and district administrators to discuss how the data should inform program improvements. The inclusion of a K–12 advisory group is required by the state to ensure that the school-level perspective is heard by those who are preparing teachers. As a result of these meetings, such improvements have been made as changes in prospective teachers' instruction on student assessment and enhanced preparation for teaching English language learners.

Because of the K–12 advisory group's joint work with the IHE on program improvement, there is greater data-based mediation and decision making among faculty and schools, where dialogue traditionally has not existed. On top of this dialogue across levels of educational leadership *within* the state, the initiative has sparked communication *between* states, so that each can learn from the successes and challenges of the others. The initiative is based on the Performance Assessment of California's Teachers, which approximately thirty IHEs in California use to inform their program adjustments. It was then brought to Washington and adapted to the state's standards and has since been adapted by state departments of education and universities in twenty additional states from coast to coast, including New York, Massachusetts, Illinois, and Wisconsin. The goal is for the assessments to be made available to all fifty U.S. states.

Large amounts of data are collected through both the performance assessment and surveys of graduates. But key to the success of this initiative is to focus on collecting *useful data*—data that are focused on teacher learning and that will motivate the faculty without overwhelming them. The data are intended to encourage reflection on what is being taught to teacher candidates. Therefore, for example, rather than throw student test score data their way—which may or may not relate specifically to preparation program content and is unlikely to motivate them to improve their programs—they provide teacher educators with data on the skills that have been mastered by the teachers they taught. Teacher educators can then see where they have been effective and where their instruction should be modified or strengthened.

The first step in improving teacher education in this way, Zeichner says, "is for universities and schools to try to come together to discuss how the university is perceived. There needs to be a dialogue." In Washington state, this dialogue now covers the performance assessment data, follow-up survey data, and research on teacher candidates' learning that is conducted by the IHE faculty.

By promoting data-informed dialogue between stakeholder groups that focuses on connecting the spectrum of teacher issues—from licensure to dismissal or career advancement—the Teacher Performance Assessment Consortium exemplifies systems thinking in improving teacher effectiveness.

Source: K. Zeichner, director of teacher education, University of Washington, personal communication, February 25, 2010.

Reenvisioning Teacher Preparation with the Teacher Education Initiative

The Teacher Education Initiative (TEI) at the University of Michigan was developed by Deborah Ball, dean of the university's School of Education, with an ambitious goal in mind: to completely rethink the way teachers are prepared for practice. The TEI vision is a complete redesign of the University of Michigan's teacher preparation program, in the hope that this major undertaking will help move the field of education toward a consensus on exactly what is needed to adequately prepare teachers for their first day in their own classroom.

Coming to a consensus on which core practices a new teacher needs to do well to start as a competent beginner is difficult. Some value more intensive workshop settings, while others favor single "high-leverage practices." Under the TEI model, Francesca Forzani, a member of the TEI team, says: "Students would move through a sequence of learning experiences where they would have to demonstrate competencies at the conclusion of each one. . . . The trick for us is to identify what those practices are that a beginning teacher would get the most out of if he or she could do it really well."

The TEI is currently working to formulate a map of these fifteen to twenty "high-leverage practices" that would be central to the curriculum redesign. One such example includes leading a whole class discussion, and training teachers would work intensively to master that skill in a hands-on environment that incorporates practice and peer critique. Each "high-leverage practice" would be grounded in whatever subject matter the teacher preparation student was engaged in, so that both the "what to teach" and the "how to teach it" are covered.

TEI efforts to address the crucial aspect of activities and settings where this new curriculum would be played out also are under way. The initiative is studying actual, designed, and virtual settings, such as school sites, laboratory settings that can be set up on campus or elsewhere, and all other representations of a teacher's work, such as videotape of instruction, communications with students and parents, and lesson plans to formulate a picture of the entire setting in which learning takes place and how the new curriculum can change practices in all of those settings.

In his 2006 report entitled *Educating School Teachers*, Arthur Levine shared this praise for the TEI concept:

> *Deborah Ball . . . offered the most lucid and compelling explanation of what a teacher education curriculum should*

> be: . . . *a traditional subject matter major . . . combined with*
> *. . . how to enable students to learn it. The future teacher*
> *would graduate knowing what to teach and how to teach it*
> *[Levine, 2006, p. 35].*
>
> *Source:* F. Forzani, project manager, Teacher Education Initiative, personal communication, August 14, 2009.

What takes place at IHEs and alternative-route preparation programs sets the tone for the remainder of a teachers' career. By constantly striving for excellence, teacher preparation programs can instill and inspire the same mind-set in the teachers they train. Moreover, IHEs should strategically admit teacher candidates in areas of short supply to aid district recruitment efforts and develop the skill sets and expertise among teacher candidates that those working on the ground level perceive as lacking. To do this, you can encourage your IHE to consult data and communicate and collaborate with the other key stakeholder groups about who to admit and what to teach them.

Other stakeholders, particularly schools and districts, should take the initiative to reach out to IHEs and create a more seamless transition from this first stage of the career continuum to those that follow: induction, performance management, and professional development. They should play an active part in a feedback loop to inform candidate admission and instruction at the IHE level. Most important, they should monitor what their teachers know after preparation and serve as instructional leaders to help teachers master what they do not know yet. After all, as students, it is hoped that teachers more than any other professionals do not cease learning beyond the completion of their formal courses.

Rubric 5.1. Is Your Teacher Preparation Program Connected to and Complemented by the Other Key Educator Talent Management Functions?

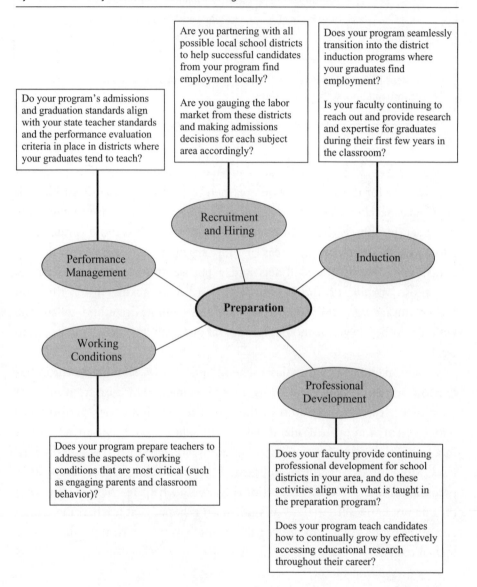

Are you partnering with all possible local school districts to help successful candidates from your program find employment locally?

Are you gauging the labor market from these districts and making admissions decisions for each subject area accordingly?

Does your program seamlessly transition into the district induction programs where your graduates find employment?

Is your faculty continuing to reach out and provide research and expertise for graduates during their first few years in the classroom?

Do your program's admissions and graduation standards align with your state teacher standards and the performance evaluation criteria in place in districts where your graduates tend to teach?

Recruitment and Hiring

Induction

Performance Management

Preparation

Working Conditions

Professional Development

Does your program prepare teachers to address the aspects of working conditions that are most critical (such as engaging parents and classroom behavior)?

Does your faculty provide continuing professional development for school districts in your area, and do these activities align with what is taught in the preparation program?

Does your program teach candidates how to continually grow by effectively accessing educational research throughout their career?

FROM HIGHER EDUCATION TO YOUR SCHOOL: GETTING THE BALL ROLLING

1. Professor Deborah Ball, the dean of the University of Michigan's School of Education, created the Teacher Education Initiative to strategically identify and change the curriculum to emphasize key high-leverage practices. Do you know of similar initiatives taking place in the teacher preparation programs that your teachers tend to graduate from? How could leaders in your school or district help forward-thinking teacher educators revamp their programs in a way that would be most useful from your perspective?

2. Washington state is at the forefront of the Teacher Performance Assessment Consortium, working with state departments of education and advisory groups of K–12 teachers, principals, and districts to more rigorously assess teachers and use this data to inform preparation program improvements. The performance data, however, are not currently used for teacher hiring. Do the teacher preparation programs in your area collect such data? If so, would the data be useful to you in informing your hiring decisions? What would be the pros and cons of applying teacher performance assessment data collected by IHEs to your hiring process?

3. Anissa Listak, managing director of Urban Teacher Residency United, noted that the residencies' ability to help districts "home-grow" the types of teachers that are needed is a useful attribute. What kind of feedback loop exists between you and those that prepare many of your teachers to allow you to provide feedback on which types of teachers to recruit and admit to the program? Which types of teachers, in terms of subject areas, grade levels, and demographic characteristics, are in short supply in your school and district?

HOW ARE THE TEACHER PREPARATION PROGRAMS THAT YOUR SCHOOL RELIES ON DOING?

A. Pedagogical Training	Yes	No	N/A
1. Do the teacher preparation programs you rely on utilize a variety of pedagogical approaches to develop teacher candidates' pedagogical expertise?	☐	☐	☐
Do they encourage coherence between academic course work and clinical experience to help candidates make connections between theory and practice?	☐	☐	☐
Do they utilize any of the following tools?	☐	☐	☐
a. Case-study methods	☐	☐	☐
b. Practitioner research	☐	☐	☐
c. Video and hypermedia materials	☐	☐	☐
d. Laboratory experiences	☐	☐	☐
e. Teacher logs, journals, diaries, reflective reports, or autobiographical sketches	☐	☐	☐
2. Do the teacher preparation programs you rely on promote the development of teacher candidates' knowledge and skills applicable to a diverse range of students and teaching settings?	☐	☐	☐
Do they require programs to actively recruit prospective teachers from diverse backgrounds?	☐	☐	☐
Do they have clinical education settings in high-needs schools, with students from diverse backgrounds?	☐	☐	☐
Do they ensure that programs utilize assessments of candidate work (such as portfolios and student work samples) that provide evidence that teacher candidates are capable of implementing differentiated instruction?	☐	☐	☐
Do they support programs that offer training in multicultural awareness?	☐	☐	☐
Do they encourage collaboration between general education and special education programs?	☐	☐	☐
3. Do the teacher preparation programs you rely on work collaboratively with you to ensure that pedagogical knowledge, content knowledge, and pedagogical content knowledge and teaching beliefs taught reflect a productive feedback loop between themselves and local schools and districts?	☐	☐	☐

	Yes	No	N/A
Do they partake in or attempt to create PK–16 partnerships?	☐	☐	☐
Do they partake in a PK–12 school advisory board or council for teacher education (if appropriate)?	☐	☐	☐
Do they select clinical placements based on potential for alignment with their vision of excellent teaching?	☐	☐	☐
B. Admissions	**Yes**	**No**	**N/A**
1. Are the teacher preparation programs you rely on responsive to district needs, paying particular attention to the specific subject areas in which teachers are needed most?	☐	☐	☐
Do they partake in or attempt to create a "grow-your-own" program, to match the needs of the district with the subject-area preparation of teachers?	☐	☐	☐
2. Do the teacher preparation programs you rely on have entry requirements that are selective and rigorous?	☐	☐	☐
Do they set a competitive minimum GPA requirement for all potential teacher preparation candidates entering a program?	☐	☐	☐
Do they ensure that all teacher candidates have the dispositions necessary to be high-quality and highly effective teachers?	☐	☐	☐
C. Data Use	**Yes**	**No**	**N/A**
1. Do the teacher preparation programs you rely on provide data that demonstrate program effectiveness and identify areas for continuous program improvement?	☐	☐	☐
Do they collect the following types of data?	☐	☐	☐
a. Follow-up studies of program graduates and corresponding administrators	☐	☐	☐
b. Performance assessments	☐	☐	☐
c. Portfolio evaluations	☐	☐	☐

REFERENCES

Allensworth, E., Ponisciak, S., & Mazzeo, C. (2009). *The schools teachers leave: Teacher mobility in Chicago Public Schools.* Chicago: Consortium on Chicago School Research. Retrieved September 23, 2009, from http://ccsr.uchicago.edu/publications/CCSR_Teacher_Mobility.pdf.

Alter, J., & Coggshall, J. (2009). *Teaching as a clinical practice profession: Implications for teacher preparation and state policy.* New York: New York Comprehensive Center. Retrieved October 1, 2009, from http://www.tqsource.org/publications/clinicalPractice.pdf.

Barber, M., & Mourshed, M. (2007). *How the world's best-performing school systems come out on top.* New York: McKinsey & Company. Retrieved February 6, 2009, from http://www.mckinsey.com/clientservice/socialsector/resources/pdf/Worlds_School_Systems_Final.pdf.

Barley, Z. A. (2009). Preparing teachers for rural appointments: Lessons from the mid-continent. *The Rural Educator, 30*(3), 10–15.

Behrstock, E., Drill, K., & Miller, S. (2009). *Is the supply in demand? Exploring how, when, and why teachers use research.* Naperville, IL: Learning Point Associates. Retrieved August 31, 2009, from http://www.learningpt.org/whatsnew/IstheSupplyinDemand.pdf.

Blanton, L. P., & Pugach, M. C. (2007). *Collaborative programs in general and special teacher education: An action guide for higher education and state policy makers.* Washington, DC: Council of Chief State School Officers. Retrieved February 6, 2009, from http://www.ccsso.org/content/pdfs/CPGSTE%20Action%20Guide%20PDF%20Final.pdf.

Bouck, E. C. (2005). Secondary special educators: Perspectives of preservice preparation and satisfaction. *Teacher Education and Special Education, 28*(2), 125–140.

Coggshall, J., & Lasagna, M. (2009). *Toward the structural transformation of schools: Innovations in staffing.* Naperville, IL: Learning Point Associates. Retrieved February 24, 2010, from http://www.learningpt.org/expertise/educatorquality/resources/publications/InnovationsInStaffing.pdf.

Darling-Hammond, L., & Baratz-Snowden, J. (2005). *A good teacher in every classroom: Preparing the highly qualified teacher our children deserve.* San Francisco: Jossey-Bass.

DeAngelis, K., Peddle, M., Trott, C., & Bergeron, L. (2002). *Teacher supply in Illinois: Evidence from the Illinois Teacher Study* (Policy Research Report). Edwardsville, IL: Illinois Education Research Council. Retrieved February 8, 2010, from http://ierc.siue.edu/documents/kdReport1202_Teacher_Supply.pdf.

Ingersoll, R., & Smith, T. (2003). The wrong solution to the teacher shortage. *Educational Leadership, 60*(8), 30–33. Retrieved February 8, 2010, from http://www.gse.upenn.edu/pdf/rmi/EL_TheWrongSolution_to_theTeacherShortage.pdf.

Kavale, K. A. (2005). Effective intervention for students with specific learning disability: The nature of special education. *Learning Disabilities, 13*(4), 127–138.

Levine, A. (2006). *Educating school teachers*. Washington, DC: The Education Schools Project. Retrieved February 6, 2009, from http://www.edschools.org/pdf/Educating _Teachers_Report.pdf.

Lucas, S. (2009, June). *Prepared for success? Results from the first four years of the Illinois Teacher Graduate Assessment Project*. Paper presented at the Illinois Education Research Symposium, Springfield, IL.

National Clearinghouse for English Language Acquisition (2010). *Frequently asked questions*. Retrieved February 24, 2010, from http://www.ncela.gwu.edu/faqs.

National Comprehensive Center for Teacher Quality & Public Agenda (2007). *They're not little kids anymore: The special challenges of new teachers in high schools and middle schools* (Issue No. 1 of *Lessons learned: New teachers talk about their jobs, challenges, and long-range plans*). New York: Public Agenda. Retrieved February 8, 2010, from http://www.tqsource.org/publications/LessonsLearned1.pdf.

National Comprehensive Center for Teacher Quality & Public Agenda (2008). *Lessons learned: New teachers talk about their jobs, challenges, and long-range plans* (Issue No. 3 of *Teaching in changing times*). New York: Public Agenda. Retrieved February 24, 2010, from http://www.publicagenda.org/files/pdf/lessons_learned_3.pdf.

National Council for Accreditation of Teacher Education. (2008). *Professional standards for the accreditation of teacher preparation institutions*. Washington, DC: Author. Retrieved February 6, 2009, from http://www.ncate.org/documents/ standards/NCATE%20Standards%202008.pdf.

Public Agenda & Learning Point Associates. (2009). *Retaining teacher talent*. Naperville, IL, and New York: Authors.

Reschly, D. J., & Bergstrom, M. K. (2009). Response to intervention. In T. B. Gutkin & C. R. Reynolds (Eds.), *The handbook of school psychology* (4th ed., pp. 434–460). New York: Wiley.

Reschly, D. J., Holdheide, L., Behrstock, E., & Weber, G. (2009). *Enhancing teacher preparation, development, and support*. In L. Goe (Ed.), *America's opportunity: Teacher effectiveness and equity in K–12 classrooms* (pp. 41–64). Washington, DC: National Comprehensive Center for Teacher Quality. Retrieved March 3, 2010, from http://www.tqsource.org/publications/2009TQBiennial/2009BiennialReport _Ch2.pdf.

Singh, D. K., & Stoloff, D. (2008). Assessment of teacher dispositions. *College Student Journal, 42*(4), 1169–1180.

Snelgrove, E. (2009, December 13). Hard lessons ahead for teachers seeking jobs in Valley. *Yakima Herald Republic*. Retrieved February 24, 2010, from http:// www.allbusiness.com/education-training/teaching-teachers-primary/13597290–1 .html.

Walsh, K., & Jacobs, S. (2007). *Alternative certification isn't alternative.* Washington, DC: National Council on Teacher Quality & Thomas B. Fordham Institute. Retrieved March 3, 2010, from http://www.nctq.org/p/publications/docs/Alternative_Certification_Isnt_Alternative_20071124023109.pdf

Whitten, E., & Rodriguez-Campos, L. (2003, Spring). Trends in the special education teaching force: Do they reflect legislative mandates and legal requirements? *Educational Horizons.* Retrieved February 24, 2010, from http://www.pilambda.org/horizons/v81–3/Whitten_Rodriguez-Campos.pdf.

Conclusion
Managing Educator Talent for Gen Y Teachers and Beyond

Today, more than ever, there is a moral and practical urgency to ensure that the right teachers and leaders are paired with the students who have been shortchanged by the American education system for too long. Jim Collins's 2001 review of how good companies become great demonstrates that "getting the right people on the bus" and into the right seats are necessary prerequisites to improving performance. Throughout this book we've emphasized the central role of the school principal, and we hope we've succeeded in helping you better understand who should be driving the bus. A 2009 briefing paper by Harvard's Susan Moore Johnson provides additional examples of the need to divest more accountability to the school level if we want investments in recruiting and retaining talented teachers to have a measurable impact on student learning. Johnson argues that every investment in a teacher's career, especially in high-need and low-performing schools—from recruitment to hiring to compensation—requires increasing the professional capacity of schools.

Nevertheless, despite the central role school leaders play in recruiting and retaining effective teachers, they cannot accomplish the task completely on their own. School leaders in partnership with the other stakeholder groups identified throughout the book—district leaders, unions, institutions of higher education, and state policymakers—must work together to identify the areas of greatest educational need, as well as what combination of policy levers will result in the very best teacher for every child. Moreover, because every school, district, and state political context is different, lasting reforms that touch on every aspect of teacher talent management and development need multiple stakeholder groups to come together time and again.

In addition to the new urgency permeating education reform conversations focused on widespread improvements to teacher effectiveness that are intended to stem the loss of another generation of young minds—particularly the minds of poor and minority children—is the generational divide occurring among the teaching force currently employed in schools and districts across the country. Sweeping demographic changes are putting more Generation Y (Gen Y) teachers—those currently under the age of thirty-three—in classrooms than ever before. According to analyses conducted by the National Commission on Teaching and America's Future (2008, p. 2), over 50 percent of the nation's educators are Baby Boomers, and as many as half of today's teachers age fifty and older (1.7 million) will likely retire in less than a decade. As a result, Gen Y teachers constitute an increasingly significant proportion of the teaching workforce, leading to a whole new set of challenges for schools and districts around new teacher support and retention.

For example, members of Gen Y are technology natives who expect that teamwork and collaboration with colleagues will be a part of any job. Just as they expect flexibility from many of the products they grew up buying, they also expect flexibility at work to create a customizable work schedule that provides a healthy balance between their personal and professional lives. Having lived with "helicopter parents" who closely monitored their progress, Gen Y members crave regular, detailed feedback from their superiors that will help them achieve their professional goals. Alongside these goals, they strive to improve their workplace and see to it that their daily job also contributes to wider positive societal change. A large majority of Gen Y teachers joined the profession specifically to help put underprivileged children on the path to success. In contrast with their concern for promoting a more open, tolerant, educated society, Gen Y members are somewhat more individualistic in their approach to rewards and sanctions for job performance, resulting in greater openness to merit pay and support for career advancement that is based more on individual performance than seniority. They are highly committed to education, but at the same time have no expectation to work for a single employer for their entire career. There is much room, therefore, for employers to understand and adapt to the preferences and priorities of this incoming cohort of young teachers (Coggshall, Behrstock, Lasagna, & Ott, 2009).

Demographic shifts in both the student population and the teaching force necessitate the development of constantly evolving talent management solutions that are comprehensive, strategic, and aligned along the eight components of the educator's career continuum—preparation, recruitment, hiring, induction, professional development, working conditions, compensation, and performance management—as opposed to the incremental and disconnected changes favored in the past. For example, as schools and districts increasingly experiment with new approaches to teacher compensation, they quickly realize that high-stakes decisions around teacher pay cannot be fairly implemented without robust measures of performance that are aligned to ongoing opportunities for professional development and better working conditions. This example illustrates the systemic nature of teacher quality reforms and the difficulty of isolating one reform component from the others along the educator's career continuum (see Rubric C.1). Throughout this book we have woven together examples of research-based strategies and systemic approaches to improving teacher quality in practice that place the school leader at the center of the reform effort.

CONDITIONS THAT SUPPORT EFFECTIVE TEACHERS AND LEADERS

We began our discussion of systemically improving teacher quality in Chapter One by focusing on the school-level strategies to improve teacher working conditions that are well within the reach of a school principal's authority. Following are some examples:

- Principal Cathy Tomon in Newport, North Carolina, demonstrated how creating a **collaborative, trustworthy, and positive school culture** can lead to a learning environment where teachers can't wait to get to work every day, where effective instructional practices are regularly shared, and where teacher retention increases dramatically.

Rubric C.1. Is Your Plan for Managing Educator Talent in Line with the Needs of the Next Generation?

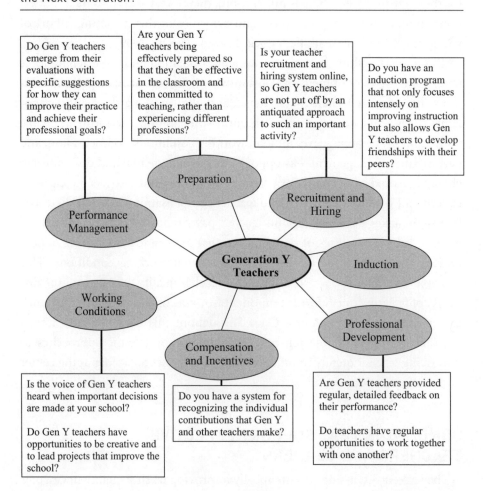

Do Gen Y teachers emerge from their evaluations with specific suggestions for how they can improve their practice and achieve their professional goals?

Are your Gen Y teachers being effectively prepared so that they can be effective in the classroom and then committed to teaching, rather than experiencing different professions?

Is your teacher recruitment and hiring system online, so Gen Y teachers are not put off by an antiquated approach to such an important activity?

Do you have an induction program that not only focuses intensely on improving instruction but also allows Gen Y teachers to develop friendships with their peers?

Preparation

Recruitment and Hiring

Performance Management

Generation Y Teachers

Induction

Working Conditions

Compensation and Incentives

Professional Development

Is the voice of Gen Y teachers heard when important decisions are made at your school?

Do Gen Y teachers have opportunities to be creative and to lead projects that improve the school?

Do you have a system for recognizing the individual contributions that Gen Y and other teachers make?

Are Gen Y teachers provided regular, detailed feedback on their performance?

Do teachers have regular opportunities to work together with one another?

- At Freedom Elementary School in Allen County, Ohio, the principal embraced the need to **engage families and the community in a meaningful and genuine way** by creating a Community Table that brought together teachers, students, parents, and community-based organizations in regular conversation to jointly identify collaborative approaches to move the school off of Academic Emergency. One of the first priorities was to ensure that **teachers' workloads are reasonable** and to brainstorm how parents and community-based organizations could provide teachers with support with the noninstructional tasks that take up so much teacher time and energy that could otherwise be focused on instruction.

- Also in Ohio, an innovative partnership between a handful of schools, the district, a local university, and an education consulting organization resulted in the adoption of a school reform model that addresses teachers' desires to **work in a safe, clean, and well-equipped facility**, but more important, it connects multiple components along the educator's career continuum. The end result is a collaborative environment created by investing in meaningful professional learning opportunities paired with differentiated reward structures for teachers who take on leadership roles and additional responsibilities and demonstrate improvements in student performance.

We began the book with a discussion of working conditions because in many instances school-level challenges such as addressing teachers' feeling of isolation or underappreciation do not require new financial resources to address: solutions are well within the range of an effective school principal's authority, especially when parents and community members are brought in to help problem-solve. Initiating large-scale teacher quality reforms with an emphasis on improving working conditions also promotes trust among the teaching faculty that their voices matter and additional reforms will be done *with* them and not *to* them. Opportunities to collaborate and to participate in decision making are particularly important school-level characteristics for Gen Y teachers (Coggshall, Behrstock, et. al., 2009, p. 23) that principals can address through creative solutions to time and staffing. However, in the end teachers of all generations consistently prefer schools that provide professional support and where working conditions support their ability to be effective with their students.

TEACHER RECRUITMENT, HIRING, AND PLACEMENT

Poor working conditions are the most often cited factor leading teachers to leave their school, district, or the profession, but collegiality, trust, feelings of isolation, and many other working condition issues can be addressed only if the right kinds of teachers are "on the bus" at each and every school. Chapter Two therefore looked at how school principals and district leaders can effectively recruit, hire, and place effective teachers as part of a systemic process of managing educator talent. Following are some specific examples:

- In Vancouver, Washington, a **values-based teacher hiring system** helped the district identify the types of teacher candidates most likely to possess certain "unteachable" values that they viewed as critical for being an effective teacher. By developing a **school leader competency model** and ensuring that school leaders who possessed these competencies played an active outreach role in teacher recruitment, the district further attracted the types of effective teachers it sought. As a consequence, teacher retention and student achievement improved, while the number of disciplinary problems decreased.

- In as urban a district as New York City and as rural an area as the Arkansas Delta Region, **targeted advertising campaigns** for the teaching profession were sponsored alongside other innovative educator talent management strategies. These billboards, subway and bus stop shelter signs, television ads, job fair displays, and web sites reminded members of the public of all ages that teaching can offer a very fulfilling career for those entering the labor market for the first time, as well as for more seasoned professionals who are changing careers.

- In the Recovery School District of New Orleans, the New Teacher Project's teachNOLA initiative provides **a model recruitment approach that is comprehensive and strategic** in its effort to attract excellent teachers whose teaching mission aligns with that of the district. Through quick responses to enquiries and other excellent customer service with candidates, they generate more and more interest in their schools during the course of the recruitment and hiring processes, demonstrating that even in the wake of highly challenging circumstances for a school and district, with the right recruitment approach it is possible to attract excellent teachers.

More than any other component, teacher recruitment highlights the systemic nature of educator talent management and the need for multiple stakeholders to work in tandem. For example, the development of partnerships with the large pool of recruits emerging from preparation programs shows the obvious connection between the preparation and recruitment phases, as well as the need for collaboration between institutions of higher education and the district and school leaders involved in teacher recruitment and hiring. At the same time, one of the first questions these recruits ask their interviewers is whether or not an induction and mentoring program will be offered to help them get up to speed with their instruction more quickly. Compensation levels, working conditions, and professional development opportunities are also considerations for teacher candidates as they choose which positions to apply for.

To avoid perpetuating inequities in the distribution of effective teachers between poor and minority children and other children, these policies must be equally attractive, if not more so, in the schools that face the greatest obstacles to student learning to entice enough excellent teachers to take on more challenging assignments. In addition to district and school policies, state-level activities can enhance the ability of schools and districts to offer the supports, salaries, and other resources that will entice more effective teachers into the schools that most need them, and more highly capable teachers to the profession. A final connection across the spectrum of educator talent management policy areas is that a strong teacher evaluation system can be used to inform and align with teacher hiring selection rubrics to create cohesive and clear expectations and secure an element of confidence that all new hires will meet these expectations and will not subsequently be found to be ineffective.

TEACHER PERFORMANCE MANAGEMENT

Now that we've got the right people on the bus and assigned to what we believe are the right seats, what individual and schoolwide performance targets should principals be setting, and how should success be measured? For too long educators have relied on the mantra, "you know good teaching when you see it," without being able to connect observations of instructional practice to some form of measurable impact on student performance. By and large, school boards, unions, and school and district administrators have focused on teacher credentials and years of experience as a proxy for effectiveness and the basis for decisions around tenure and compensation. The field of teacher evaluation was also largely untapped by the education research and development community, with few valid and reliable measures of teacher performance—based on observations or formative assessment of student growth—for school and district leaders to choose from. However, a number of recent education reform trends—including an increased emphasis on data to inform instructional practice, more accountability for achievement at every level and for every subgroup, experimentation with compensation reform, and the overwhelming research pointing to the direct and measurable impact teachers have on student achievement—has led to a national conversation about the need to restructure teacher evaluation as part of a larger effort to rethink performance management in education.

While principals have historically had primary responsibility for monitoring effective teaching, district and union leadership set the parameters for what can and cannot be addressed, as well as how and when evaluations should occur. In addition, because in most cases the results of teacher evaluations are not tied to other performance management strategies such as tenure and compensation, evaluations are conducted infrequently and without much concern for rigor. The current emphasis on reforming how teachers are evaluated and compensated opens the door for exciting new conversations among school and district leaders about how best to identify and reward the most effective talent, how to provide targeted support and incentives for teachers in the middle who want to improve, and how to fairly and consistently move ineffective teachers out of the classroom. Recent research on Gen Y teachers' attitudes toward aligning compensation with differentiated roles, responsibilities, and teacher effectiveness provides further ammunition for schools and districts to undertake this conversation. The desire for frequent feedback from school leaders as part of a continuous formative evaluation process is a high priority for Gen Y teachers. They are also increasingly open to performance-based pay structures, but they do not trust the use of annual student achievement tests as a basis for differentiating performance. Gen Y teachers want to see a valid and reliable approach to differentiating quality teaching (Coggshall, Behrstock, et. al., 2009).

In response to emerging trends in federal policy priorities and more receptivity to performance management reforms in the teaching force, Chapter Three examined the enduring role of unions in a changing performance management landscape and provided examples of fair and equitable approaches to evaluation and compensation. A fair and equitable performance management system includes a teacher evaluation process that engages teachers, unions, and school and district leaders. A robust approach to performance management connects multiple components along the educator's career continuum, beginning with professional learning opportunities that tie performance-based feedback to opportunities for professional growth that are aligned to school and district priorities. A systemic performance management system should also expand opportunities for teachers to take on new leadership responsibilities, and should lay the groundwork for identifying genuine differences in performance, to be addressed through the provision of more support for struggling teachers or celebrated and differentially compensated in the case of highly effective teachers. Following are examples of **systemic and more robust approaches to performance management**, which were illustrated in the vignettes in Chapter Three:

- As president of the Minneapolis Federation of Teachers #59, Lynn Nordgren has been a persistent advocate for improving student growth by promoting higher standards of performance and better compensating teachers who meet those standards. Over time, Nordgren has worked to align achievement of tenure, peer review as part of teacher evaluation, professional development, and differentiated compensation, to form a truly systemic package of performance management reforms.

- Similarly, in Fairfax County, Virginia, district officials embarked on a reform effort to more effectively deploy their teaching talent in the core content areas and adjust compensation to reward teachers for taking on greater responsibility for student learning, working in teams, and taking initiative to grow their knowledge and skills in alignment with district goals.

As we demonstrated through examples of emerging policy and practice in Chapter Three, it takes work to maximize the teaching talent in a school or district. No part of a reform initiative exists in a vacuum, and whether the impetus for creating a more robust approach to performance management is born within the central office, the principal's office, or the local union head-quarters, all parties must be mission driven and begin from a shared set of values on what is best for students as the primary outcome.

ENABLING TEACHERS, BUILDING THE PROFESSION

School leaders directly influence multiple aspects of teacher retention, including the ability to create a supportive workplace and the ongoing assessment of teacher knowledge to identify the most appropriate professional development opportunities that will allow the novice teacher to continue to grow in confidence and skill. Nevertheless, a cacophony of local governance structures complicated by state and federal education mandates often interfere with the principal's authority to influence local reform efforts. Rather than giving up as a result of the complex web of policies, players, and practices, principals should engage in local and state-level policy conversations—especially if the end result is the possibility of additional funding to support ongoing teacher development. The key to effectively engaging in state and local policy conversations is better understanding the parameters of what can and cannot be accomplished through state interventions, such as the following:

- States develop policies that set the parameters for funding, implementation, and quality.
- State education agency staff can provide guidance to schools and districts, as well as access to resources that can inform the content of

teacher development—from preparation to induction to ongoing professional development.

- States influence local school and district access to federal funding.

Chapter Four examined two successful examples of state-led and -financed education initiatives that support school and district leadership reforms around **high-quality induction, mentoring, and professional development,** as follows:

- With the explicit goal of "assisting with the development and retention of highly qualified teachers in Hawaii's public schools," state legislation beginning in 2005 and reinforced in 2009 established guidelines for teacher induction and mentoring in each of Hawaii's school "complexes" or districts. As each school complex began to tackle implementation of the new teacher induction and mentoring policy, a local education organization joined the rollout and added a professional development component that assigned "cultural mentors" to new teachers along with their traditional content-based mentors. In the fourteen complex areas where state policy, community partnerships, and local leadership have come together to address teacher retention, new teachers are acclimated to their students' communities and values, as well as to their chosen profession—and teacher turnover has slowed to a trickle.

- Maryland's Professional Development Advisory Council was charged with seeking local input on the development of quality standards for the delivery of professional development in the state. With consistent support from the state superintendent, several years later the initiative has resulted in a suite of online tools for schools and districts on how to design and implement locally relevant and high-quality professional development experiences for teachers.

In both instances, state leadership was instrumental in developing standardized practices and eventually requiring the implementation of high-quality induction, mentoring, and professional development in every school and district. School leaders can take advantage of state resources to rethink school-based teacher retention strategies, and knowledge of state policy and available funding is useful ammunition when requesting additional district-level support.

One critical state policy lever that often impedes the reallocation of school-level resources is laws mandating the amount of instructional time in the core content areas. Opportunities for teachers to collaborate across subject areas, grade levels, or around targeted student needs are often difficult for school leaders to create as a result. Increasingly, however, examples of creative approaches to differentiating school-staffing patterns are changing the historic "egg-crate" approach to teaching and learning in schools (Coggshall, Lasagna, & Laine, 2009; Silva, 2009; Hassel & Hassel, 2010). Innovative school and district leaders who are knowledgeable about both the opportunities and constraints that come with state policy, and who are attuned to the latest developments in the effective use of time and staffing can create regularly scheduled adult learning opportunities during the school day that benefit student growth and development.

THE ROLE OF INSTITUTIONS OF HIGHER EDUCATION IN PREPARING TEACHERS FOR SUCCESS

This book ends with the beginning of the teacher career continuum: preparation and the role of institutions of higher education and alternative route programs. Chapter Five establishes how preparation—though often seen as disconnected from other teacher recruitment, development, and retention policies—is an integral component of teacher quality policy reform.

Teacher preparation programs serve as a gateway to the profession, determining which types of teachers join the profession from the start. In a study of the world's best school systems, McKinsey & Company found that more selective systems for admitting candidates to teacher preparation programs set apart countries with strong teacher workforces by sending a signal to college graduates about who ought to consider teaching as a career and raising the prestige of teaching in the minds of top students (Barber and Mourshed, 2007). In addition to limiting potential teachers to highly talented candidates, preparation programs can limit the new teacher pool to those teachers with expertise in the subject areas that are in short supply, such as math, science, foreign languages, and special education—particularly if they are willing to teach in high-need, hard-to-staff schools or neighborhoods.

Of course, teacher preparation programs also contribute greatly to a new teacher's effectiveness once in the classroom. The academic and practical training they provide equip teachers with critical knowledge and skills, including identifying students' challenges and differentiating instruction to meet the unique needs of students, implementing evidence-based practices and using research to continually advance their repertoire of teaching strategies, engaging with parents, and effectively managing classroom behavior. By doing or failing to do these things effectively, teacher preparation programs set the tone for the remainder of the teachers' careers, strongly influencing whether teachers see themselves as having entered a mission-driven, professional, respected, strong, and effective profession or not.

Chapter Five discussed the following innovations in teacher preparation aimed at strengthening the profession:

- At the University of Michigan, Dean of the School of Education Deborah Ball led the development of the Teacher Education Initiative, which uses **high-leverage practices** and the demonstration of competencies around them to frame the teacher preparation curriculum. This complete redesign of the curriculum directs resources toward the fifteen to twenty elements of preparation that most strongly affect classroom effectiveness, and students are now benefiting as a result of the enhanced knowledge and skill of teachers who are new to the classroom.

- Leaders at the University of Washington and Stanford University worked with a consortium of state, district, and school leaders to develop Teacher Performance Assessment **instruments to evaluate teacher effectiveness** across the continuum—when they are entering the profession, being evaluated to identify areas for growth, and when other decisions such as tenure are made. Leaders in institutions of higher education and leaders from schools and other stakeholder groups then use the data to spark dialogue about areas for improvement for individual teacher preparation programs, so that they can better meet the needs of schools for effective teachers for all students. Already this initiative is spreading across twenty states around the country.

- From coast to coast, urban teacher residency programs are rising to plug holes in the existing teacher pipeline. Anissa Listak was a leading force behind the growth of urban teacher residencies. Among other things, the residency programs confer with school districts about their current needs for teachers for the different subject areas, grade levels, and other groupings. By listening to leaders at the ground level share their specific needs for new teachers, these urban teacher residencies both bridge the divide between the different players in the education arena and address the need to recruit not just more teachers, but more of the right kinds of teachers.

School leaders should recognize that although much of what happens in teacher preparation is outside their purview, they—not the teacher candidates themselves—are the ultimate "client" for institutions of higher education and alternative route preparation programs, and their voice in the content of teacher preparation can and should be a prominent one. School leaders should actively facilitate reforms in teacher preparation with the range of stakeholders, because no single stakeholder group can change the system alone. At the same time, those leading teacher preparation recognize that school leaders—because they are closest to students and to teachers—are best positioned to inform and advise on changes to policy and practice that will strengthen the teaching profession and the education system for all students now and for the future.

There are no shortcuts for achieving sustainable improvements to teacher quality. The nature of the teaching profession is one of ongoing learning aligned with continuous changes in the complex fabric of our twenty-first-century society, where education is at the heart of all that is possible in this century and the next. The role of teachers in molding the next generation of great minds, who will contribute to innovations in every aspect of our daily lives, should not be underestimated. This enormous responsibility is why investments in teacher quality reforms are critical to the survival of the education enterprise, and why stakeholders at every level of the system need to come together to think holistically about improvements to the teacher's career continuum. School leaders are at the center of the reform conversation as they interact with students and teachers on the ground every day, yet have the opportunity at every level of the system to influence decisions about the future of teaching. Leaders who choose to accept the strategies and recommendations for improving teacher quality described in this book are far more likely to achieve lasting reforms that change the face of teaching and learning for the good of each and every child.

REFERENCES

Barber, M., & Mourshed, M. (2007). *How the world's best-performing school systems come out on top*. New York: McKinsey & Company. Retrieved February 6, 2009, from http://www.mckinsey.com/clientservice/socialsector/resources/pdf/Worlds_School_Systems_Final.pdf.

Collins, J. (2001). *Good to great*. Retrieved August 21, 2009, from http://www.jimcollins.com/article_topics/articles/good-to-great.html.

Coggshall, J., Behrstock, E., Lasagna, M. & Ott, A. (2009). *Supporting teacher effectiveness: The view from Generation Y*. Naperville, IL: Learning Point Associates.

Coggshall, J., Lasagna, M., & Laine, S. (2009). *Toward the structural transformation of schools: Innovations in staffing*. Naperville, IL: Learning Point Associates.

Hassel, B., & Hassel, E. A. (2010). *Opportunity at the top: How America's best teachers could close the gaps, raise the bar, and keep our nation great*. Chapel Hill, NC: Public Impact.

Moore Johnson, S. (2009). *How best to add value: Strike a balance between the individual and the organization in school reform*. Washington, DC: Economic Policy Institute.

National Commission on Teaching and America's Future. (2008). *Learning teams: Creating what's next*. Washington, DC: Author.

Silva, E. (2009). *Teachers at work: Improving teacher quality through school design*. Washington, DC: Education Sector.

Index